MARCHING TO A DIFFERENT DRUMMER

Martin Goldfarb & Thomas Axworthy

MARCHING TO A DIFFERENT DRUMMER

AN ESSAY ON THE LIBERALS AND CONSERVATIVES IN CONVENTION

First published in 1988 by
Stoddart Publishing Co. Limited
34 Lesmill Road
Toronto, Canada
M3B 2T6

Canadian Cataloguing in Publication Data

Goldfarb, Martin
   Marching to a different drummer: an essay on the
    Liberals and Conservatives in convention

ISBN 0-7737-2230-0

1. Progressive Conservative Party of Canada.
2. Liberal Party of Canada.   3. Canada – Politics and
government – 1963-   – Public opinion.
4. Public opinion – Canada.   5. Public opinion polls.
I. Axworthy, Tom, 1947-   II. Title.

JL196.G64 1988   320.5'0971   C88-095003-X

Printed and bound in the United States

For Joan and Roberta

Table of Contents

Acknowledgments

Acknowledgments account only for the debts one remembers. We cannot fully express here the appreciation we owe to the hundreds of friends and colleagues from all parties, who have tutored us in the mysteries of politics.

To Ellen Karp, Paul Myles and Barbara Berketta of Goldfarb Consultants we owe a special debt for the time and expertise they so freely gave. The entire team at Goldfarb Consultants deserves our thanks for their professionalism in collecting the data which forms the core of this book.

The Center of International Affairs at Harvard University provided a collegial setting in which to write and the director, Sam Huntington, was gracious with his hospitality and advice. Louise Jennings, while helping to coordinate the Canadian-American seminar series at Harvard, also assisted us in organizing several of the chapters. Joan Goldfarb and Roberta Axworthy gave the manuscript a much needed editing, and Anne Marriott worked on the final compilation in her usual competent way.

Professor George Perlin of Queen's University is an old friend and colleague who assisted us in a most material way by graciously giving permission to compare in tabular form our 1983 and 1984 data with his survey findings which go back to 1967. McGill-Queen's Press, publisher of Professor Perlin's *The Tory Syndrome* also gave their permission to reproduce this information, and for this we are thankful.

Professor Hugh Thorburn of Queen's University was equally kind in letting us cite data from a 1970 unpublished paper on the policy preferences of Conservative and Liberal party delegates.

Finally, we owe a particular debt of gratitude to a special friend. Keith Davey was instrumental in introducing both of us to the Liberal party, and we are indebted to him for his many acts of kindness over the years.

Authors' Note

Rarely since the creation of the country has Canada's political future been so unclear. The Conservative party, triumphant in 1984, is promoting (through its policies of free trade with the United States and the Meech Lake Constitutional Accord) an activist agenda, but has been mired in third place throughout much of its mandate. The Liberal party's star is beginning once again to rise, but amidst uncertainty and debate. Finally, the shadow of the NDP hovers over the Conservatives and the Liberals, with the social democrats poised perhaps for their long-awaited breakthrough.

Our thesis is straightforward: something dramatic has happened to Canadian party politics since the 1960s. Twenty years ago, it was popularly understood that the two major parties were ideologically quite similar. Today, the Liberals and Conservatives are ideologically distinctive. The Liberals have become more liberal and the Conservatives have become more conservative.

The effect of this divergence of ideologies is now having an influence on politics. The Meech Lake Accord and the free trade debate, two of the most controversial issues in the history of Canadian politics, originated in this division over values.

This book, written by a pollster and a former Liberal party activist, is about parties and leadership. It attempts to make sense of 1988's murky political waters, at a time when Canadians soon will be asked once again to make choices about issues, parties and leadership. When Canadians think about politics, leadership dominates their perspective. For most Canadians, the leader is the party. This study is about leadership. More precisely, it is about how Canada's two major parties go about choosing a leader.

On June 11, 1983 and June 16, 1984, respectively, the Conservative and Liberal parties of Canada convened to choose new leadership. Within those dramatic 12 months, the lengthy era of Pierre Elliott Trudeau came to a close, the Conservative delegates overthrew Joe Clark and selected Brian Mulroney, and the Liberal party spurned Jean Chrétien in favor of its long-awaited crown prince, John Turner. Then, on November 30, 1986, the Liberals once again renewed their faith in their leader.

This is not a blow-by-blow insider's account of a fascinating period in Canadian political history. Many such accounts already have been written and undoubtedly more are on the way.[1] Nor is this study concerned with the September 4, 1984 general election, except insofar as the factors that influence leadership choice may play a role in how the parties run a campaign. The focus of this study is the several thousand Canadians who attended those conventions in Ottawa. These men and women are the party activists and they form one side of the triangle that makes up a political party.

Prior to these conventions, Goldfarb Consultants was retained by the CTV network to do a survey of delegate voting intentions and attitudes toward the issues of the day.[2] This data helped CTV to inform Canadians about what was taking place on the convention floor. But beyond their use as a prop in electronic journalism, the surveys provided a rare snapshot of the Conservative and Liberal parties at work.

The authors, convinced that the convention process is something that is little understood, have decided to share these convention snapshots with all Canadians in order to demonstrate the unique insights they provide about how the political process functions. These snapshots describe the players and delineate what each of the parties represents in terms of values and political philosophy. The book opens with a discussion by Martin Goldfarb about the controversial role of the pollster in the contemporary political spectrum.

Introduction

MARTIN GOLDFARB

One of the most controversial figures in the constellation of contemporary political life is the public opinion pollster. Yet the role of the pollster in today's political arena is expanding continually. Like any seer or oracle, the pollster plays a role that is viewed with a combination of respect, fear, intrigue and controversy. The following chapters bring insight to contemporary politics based on data culled from polls. They interpret history from both the scientific and artistic perspectives of the pollster. Before we turn to that data, however, we must reflect briefly on the role of the pollster in Canadian politics.

We live in the world of the information blitz. Information, constant but ever-changing, comes so quickly that to absorb it all is impossible. But for the ordinary citizen to feel involved in this process, he must absorb, analyze and apply this information. It is in this context that the pollster has been thrust forward as a notable figure in the new political arena.

Polls provide an instant means for the individual to identify himself on the scale of public opinion. Polling belongs to the world of universal democracy. The process enables citizens to understand where their opinions and values fit in the range of attitudes about issues that affect their lives and their country. Polls are not plebiscites, but function in a similar manner: they provide instant feedback on the most important issues.

Polls create an involved citizenry. For the voter, polls may make the political process more gratifying, challenging and thought-provoking. As a result of polls, the individual is able to become more knowledgeable about issues confronting society and the institutions and processes that serve it.

Polls put pressure on politicians. In the shadow of public opinion and public accountability, politicians cannot lead blindly. Polls help politicians to understand public opinion and thereby to develop strategies.

In the information age, the pollster has taken on a new role, which has evolved over the last 20 years to make him or her a force in the machinery of idea generation in modern society. In politics and public policy, in product development and subsequent promotion, in image crafting and positioning, the pollster has become a quintessential contributor.

Edward L. Bernays was the founding father of American advertising, the very first presidential media advisor and — curiously — Sigmund Freud's nephew. The fundamental principle of Bernays' conceptual thinking, which he succinctly and provocatively called "The Engineering of Consent," was, in his words, "the application of scientific practices and tried practices in the task of getting people to support ideas and programs." *Engineering* implies the use of scientific methods, and *consent* means the public must be won over, not an easy task since the appeal must be constant. Consent also denotes choice — a crucial yet volatile element. It implies that people can choose to change their minds and withdraw their consent. This applies equally to selling products and to winning elections.[1]

To put it simply, Bernays wanted to translate insight into action. This is the essence of the role of polling in today's society. Unlike his uncle, Freud, who was happy to acknowledge insight for its own sake, Bernays wanted to use insight as a way of making things happen. But more than anything else, he knew that a pollster's work is an art form — not just a profession.

Rarely do people reflect deeply about what pollsters do; what roles they play in the evolution of our society; what ethics they uphold. Pollsters are seen paradoxically — simultaneously revered and reviled, praised and blamed, and mostly misunderstood by both their clients and the public.[2]

In a society insecure about the nature of political power, pollsters seem to possess a mystique. In point of fact, the techniques pollsters use to collect information are relatively simple: to collate data and generate numbers, one needs a devotion to procedure and a commitment to established practice. Similarly, there is little mysticism involved in statistical manipulation of the information that has been generated. And while the results may be startling, the process of arriving at them is not. Pollsters simply ask what they consider to be pertinent questions, then analyze and interpret the answers.

It is the interpretation of results — not the collection of data — that sets a good pollster apart from an ordinary one. There is no magical formula. As any capable cultural anthropologist knows — and a capable pollster is a sophisticated student of cultural behavior — deciphering the nuances of attitudes, opinions and behaviors in a context of cultural complexity is a difficult task. It requires intellectual instinct, intuition and an immense amount of experience. It requires a genuine intimacy with culture and sensitivity to a generation. Cultural artifacts change quickly in our age, and pollsters must be equally quick to anticipate, recognize and analyze these changes.

All pollsters, whether or not they admit it (and the good ones do!) have a value system. This is not simply a matter of personal ethics, but of awareness of the value systems of clients and of society, whether the values in question are political, corporate or any other. It is a spurious argument for pollsters to try to deny this reality. Good polling, like good art, demands and propagates certain values as opposed to others.

And so it should be! For a good pollster concludes his work by recommending or advocating certain courses of action which will either promote or prevent certain outcomes. It is also vital, however, to recognize that ethics demand that pollsters portray the reality their research has made apparent. Frequently, such a portrait may not be the one clients expect, or even want to see. That, however, is a secondary consideration. What is consistently important is that pollsters adhere to the reality, perceptions and interpretations evoked by their results.

Pollsters do not change society's behavior: this is neither their role, nor their function. They are essentially private figures who are unlikely to have any *direct* influence on the public's behavior. This is not to say, however, that a pollster's findings do not potentially influence the decisions of other individuals who do wish to affect public behavior.

There are, however, ethical questions that all pollsters face. Should we know? Should information gleaned from polling be made available? Should we find out what we don't want to know? These are questions crucial to the ethics of polling. Should politicians, for example, have access to the results of polls taken during election campaigns? Should polls form part of the context of decision making? Indeed, the formative and abiding commitment of the pollster is to discern reality, not to withhold or change the findings. Information may be used, or it may not be, depending on the individual or the situation. Pollsters, however, must be true to the portrait of reality that has emerged from their work.

The questions do not stop here. Can anyone become a client? In my view, the answer is no, and for two reasons. First, the pollster-client relationship is a very intimate one. To do a good job, a pollster must understand the perceptions, requirements, problems and difficulties of the client. If there is a fundamental clash of values between them, the results will benefit neither. Second, a pollster should never warp the results for anyone's benefit — even for a client. There must be some fundamental empathy — shared values, if you like — between pollster and client. Only with this commonality can a pollster tell a client "the way it really is," while also enabling the client to appreciate the significance and the implications of the results.

THE POLLSTER AND THE POLITICIANS

There is a crucial, and very private, relationship between the pollster and the politician, the pollster and a government and between a pollster and the governing political party. It is a truism to say that today, if you are going to succeed in securing and maintaining political power, part of the accouterment of power is the pollster. Polling today is to the politician what the stock market is to the financial analyst. It is impossible to think of the conduct of political affairs without the art and science of the pollster.

We tend to think of this relationship as a direct consequence of the information age. However, in another sense, the parallel is with the traditional and historically specific role of the advisor to the court. Throughout history, every court had a soothsayer, a prophet, a court jester, or a fool. These individuals served at the pleasure of the king or the leader. They were appointed by the king and they lived, and frequently died, with the success or the failure of the king. Historically, these figures stood as the voice of wisdom, the independent source of truth. They offered the king their views of reality, regardless of whom these revelations might offend. They stood as interpreters of public sentiment to a court and a class of nobility which was in most cases far removed from what the masses thought or felt. The court jester watched the spectacle of politics and the often bloody infighting among the nobility, and he interpreted these spectacles for the king, admonishing, counselling, advising and even warning him. Each court jester, history tells us, had his own style, his own insights, and his own unique characteristics. The fool in Shakespearian plays, for example, was the metaphysician of the court, revealing the world for what it really was. The fool always retained a measure of objectivity in court matters, for his primary duty was to speak the truth. He could never be punished for telling the truth.

It was the dynamic between the fool, or jester, and the court that made a sense of balance or justice prevail in the affairs of men. If the king simply succumbed to the nobility, naked power would prevail in court affairs. In many of Shakespeare's plays, in fact, the fool was the central character and has exerted a long-lasting fascination. We understand the king by understanding the fool.

The modern equivalent to this historical figure is the pollster. Like the historical fool, he assumes his office at the bequest of the court, or the decision-makers who hire him. His fate is tied to the success or failure of those individuals, for his star rises and falls with the success or failure of the "court" he serves. He is the court confidante and knows more about the inner machinations of his court than anybody else — maybe even more than the leader.

Today, however, there are many new dimensions to this already complex relationship.

Democracies are built on the assumption that the citizen makes decisions, usually electoral decisions, based upon information, formulating attitudes and opinions which affect the behavior patterns of the public at large.

Politicians today believe that they understand these complex patterns of attitudes, opinions and beliefs. Their confidence in a pollster's ability to identify the consensus of society gives them the impetus to rely so heavily upon polls and the individuals who create them.

But it goes even further. Politicans come to pollsters not only to find out what the public wants or thinks or feels, but also to ask the pollster what to do. The pollster, as a result, becomes involved in strategic development, action plans, guidance for political rule and even governing.

Moreover, since the issues and the agenda of public action change so quickly today, the politicians make increasing demands upon the pollster. Politicians may want to know where the public stands on issues on a day-to-day basis, and the technology of day-to-day polling is available to provide that information. It is not difficult to discern where the consensus rests on any issue. Presidents, prime ministers and others have availed themselves of this information.

The ethical question, however, remains: given poll-derived information, what course of action is legitimate? Political leaders still do, and always will, face this question: while we may know this or that, what should we do? Herein lies the art of politics. What makes the art of politics even more difficult today is the fact that more information is available. We can know more, know it more accurately and know it in greater detail! It is increasingly difficult for politicians to ignore public opinion on any given issue. The dissonance between what we know and what we should do, therefore, becomes more extreme.

The art of the pollster has made the life of politicians much more difficult, not easier. The pollster has added a new dimension of responsibility to the decisions of the politician. The crisis politicians frequently face is that while they know what may be popular, they want to act on the basis of what they think is *right* and the two are often in conflict. This is a crisis which the art of the pollster has intensified.

There is another dimension to this problem. The public, through broadcast and print reporting, is becoming increasingly aware of the results of polling. They read or hear continually about what pollsters report as the consensus on a given issue and they use this information as a basis on which to make political decisions. Voters judge politicians on the basis of this public knowledge and frequently they make some harsh and educated judgments. Hence, the growing independence of voters or the increasing volatility of the electorate may be a direct result of the pervasiveness of polling information in our society.

The information that polling, by means of the media, provides does two things. On one hand, it generates a more involved electorate. On the other, it creates a more volatile and pressure-ridden political system.

Today's politicians have access to very little information that is not also available to the public. Voters, therefore, can judge politicians' decisions on the basis of what they themselves think or might do about any political issue. As a result, they are better able to evaluate decisions made by their politicians. Voters today, by means of poll-generated information, are far better critics of the political decision-making process than those who came before.

Furthermore, politicians can no longer hide behind private information. In a world dominated by an instant and massive communications network, steered by pollsters and the media, the public now has access to information right on the heels of the politicians. This has fundamentally changed the nature of politics in our society. No longer do we see ourselves electing, or hiring, politicians as wiser, more knowledgeable sages to protect us with their deeper insight into the means of attaining the public good. They have become instead our public representatives, our public relations spokespeople. We elect our politicians to represent our values, attitudes and interests to the country and to the world at large.

Polling signals to politicians and to the public that they are playing in the same ballpark. What one knows, the other knows. What one wants, the other can engineer.

THE INFLUENCE OF THE POLLSTER

As the pollster becomes a more public figure, the extent of his or her influence reaches far beyond the confines of the pollster-patron relationship.

In political affairs, for example, the pollster now operates not only in the context of elections and electioneering, but also in relation to the formulation of policy and the implementation of policy. The pollster is a major player in all levels of government policy making. The politician, and even the civil servant, consults the pollster on an ongoing basis. While the pollster has not eclipsed more traditional instruments and institutions of policy making (in other words, members of Parliament, the caucus, the bureaucracy, the opinion leaders of society), we now have, to a degree, "government by pollster."

The pollster is also a significant figure in the legitimization of policy. He is frequently consulted for advice and counsel as to how government can sell or market its policies to the public. This process of legitimizing public policy is becoming an increasingly important and sophisticated aspect of governing. Here again, the pollster's influence is increasing.

However, the extension of the influence of the pollster in the political process, in the policy-making process and in the legitimization of policy raises some very serious questions. First, the pollster is a unique, non-elected player in the political arena. As we begin to recognize this fact, we must begin to rethink the way in which the pollster fits into the political apparatus governing our society. At the moment, neither pollsters nor politicians have given much thought to this problem but it is probably the single most revolutionary innovation in the nature of government. The pollster contributes information which is used as leverage in decision making by those with the power to do so. This is fundamental to the future of the polling profession and presumably fundamental to the future development of the political process. All must begin to consider and debate it.

There is another vital aspect to this problem. Can we say that this phenomenon, the extension of the influence of the pollster in our political process, is beneficial or detrimental to individual freedom? Does it mean that our democratic institutions are more — or less — democratic than they were, say 30 years ago? Does it make the individual voter a more responsible citizen?

The extension of the influence of the pollster has fundamentally shifted the balance in our political system to enhance and make more difficult citizens' political choices. As the pollster becomes established as a political institution in our society, and voters become more detached from traditional partisanship, they become more independent and more volatile. The problems of governing successfully become more — not less — difficult. We are entering a phase in the development of democratic citizenship where people armed with much more sophisticated information are making harsher and more analytical judgments of their politicians.

THE POLLSTER AND POLITICAL LEVERAGE

Public opinion does change, but as all political polls show, it changes rather slowly. Frequently, this rate of change is much too slow for the likes of politicians. Barring unforeseen calamities or catastrophes from which politicians cannot disassociate themselves, their ability to affect the nature of public opinion is limited. In our society, you cannot control all events, all news, nor all the ways in which the public forms opinions about its political leaders.

In spite of this, politicians can and do affect the nature of public opinion. Though this is only part of their mandate, it is becoming increasingly important. Indeed, politicians now have become *more* fixated upon affecting public opinion than upon doing what they think is right.

Politicians accomplish their manipulation of public opinion today through the notion of *leverage*. In an open-market society such as ours, individuals and groups are under enormous cross-pressures, factors which seek to affect their behavior, thoughts, attitudes, values, political preferences and so forth. One should not underestimate this vast complex of cross-pressures. (Leverage is the ability to determine the point at which, and the mechanism by which, one is able to affect an individual or group's behavior, thoughts, attitudes and values.) Timing, the medium and the message are crucial in order to lever someone's attitudes. Politics today is, more and more, the seeking out of leverage.

The one commodity increasingly at the disposal of government and politicians is information. And this information is used, more and more, as a basis of leverage in our political system. Someone who has information which another person or the electorate does not have uses this information as a basis of levering that other person toward a particular position or decision.

Polling has increasingly become the art of acquiring that vital piece of information that the other person or group does not have. This then enables the politician or party to lever public opinion in certain directions. Both the timing and the medium by which that information is communicated and the content of its messages become critical. The pollster provides the basic information from which levering strategies are fashioned.

Politicians increasingly act defensively. They do not want to do anything that may come to be considered a mistake. Ongoing paralysis of political action is one of the most perplexing realities of our politics. Politicians might readily admit that they think they know what should be done to alleviate a problem, but the fear of making a mistake, fear of a crippling error, frequently deters them from taking such actions.

The pollster, today, functions frequently to help reduce the risk of untoward actions. By providing vital information about the likely public receptivity to political policy and behavior, the pollster defines the costs and benefits of political action.

Are polls detrimental to the public good? This question has now become an ongoing preoccupation of many. Some would ban polls altogether. Others would ban polls at election time. Still others demand that all polls conducted at public expense should be made public immediately.

Society indeed has a right to know the means by which decisions made in the public interest are taken. I believe in freedom of information and public access to government documents. Hence, I believe that polls conducted as a basis of collecting information and polls used in the decision-making process of government should be made public.

Equally important in our political life, however, is the notion of responsibility. We elect politicians to conduct the affairs of our nation, province, or municipality. Politicians assume that public trust, and with it they must assume the burden of responsibility for acting in the public interest.

The increasing public posture of pollsters and the opening of access to polled information should not become a foundation for the shirking of responsibility by public officials. Politics means judgment — judgment about actions conducive to the public good. Elections are institutional mechanisms whereby we are able to define the nature of that responsibility — to heap praise and to assign the burden of blame. The pollster is not, nor should he ever become, the focus of this process of responsibility.

I believe that polling and the increased use of polling in our political life has increased the capacity of elected officials to make wise decisions. Wisdom means mature intelligence, common sense, sound judgment, perception and discretion. The pollster has provided a vehicle for pursuing, interpreting and directing action for the public good, based upon this notion of wisdom.

THE POLLSTER AND THE CHANGING NATURE OF DEMOCRACY

Information is power and political information is political power — or so goes an adage of our age.

Democracy has changed — from small-scale participatory democracy, through representative democracy, to information democracy. While we retain the institutional structures of representative democracy, it is clear that new forces, new figures and new, evolving institutions are changing our democratic processes. Information — issue specific, time specific — is now the life blood of the political process and the policy-making process of our society. The pollster is the gatekeeper of political information.

We must now begin to discuss the problem of how the pollster has affected the nature of contemporary democracy. Have we moved irrevocably away from representative democracy to a pollster/information-based democracy? What does that mean? How has the pollster transformed the elements of traditional politics: i.e., values, ideologies, personalities? Can the nature of political life be the same after the advent of the pollster? In realistic terms, to what degree is the pollster, as the gatekeeper of information, the instrument of political manipulation and control?

My experience suggests to me that the consumer and the voter bases his or her decisions on a combination of experience, fact and intuition. Individual decision making, either for consumer goods or for political leaders and parties, is becoming increasingly evaluative. People today are taking the time to make hard choices. Choice — whether to drink Pepsi or Coke, whether to vote for leader X or leader Y — is a given throughout our society. Nobody should assume that winning over a person from one soft drink to another is an easy task. It is not. Nor is winning over a person for leader X or leader Y. The process of winning individual choice today is an ongoing process. This done, it is a constant struggle to maintain a person's allegiance.

The process of winning over an individual and acquiring his allegiance is exactly what consent involves. Consent implies choice. And today, in an extremely competitive environment, winning over someone to a product or a leader is a precarious business. People are constantly being asked to change their minds and to evaluate what they are doing. They are constantly being seduced or challenged to consider the alternatives.

The pollster can help us understand how individuals make decisions and help us understand the process of choice. He or she may even be able to predict the stages in the decision-making process, but cannot predict the actual choice. By explaining to the politicians the decision-making process and its stages, a pollster can reduce the risks to the politician and increase the leverage the politician may have. But a pollster can neither determine the outcome of the political process nor predict how the voters will decide. If voters sense a lack of leadership, for example, a very rapid process of rejection sets in. One cannot predict, nor even control, what will trigger off the sense of lack of leadership.

THE POLLSTER AND THE CANADIAN VOTER

Polling has taught me many things. But probably the most important thing, the fact that all good pollsters must always keep in mind, is that the source of wisdom rests always with the consumer and the voter. The consumer and the voter react from a fundamental and deeply rooted base of common sense. In the final analysis, people vote from self-interest. They evaluate the political world and make their decision on the basis of what they think and know is best for themselves and their families. This does not mean that people are egotistical, narrow, or selfish, but rather that citizens in our society participate in a community where they recognize that choosing always means choosing the best for themselves, for their children and families, and for their community. This is what common sense means. It is a sense of what is best or what is common to all people in a community, the collective wisdom of the voter and the consumer. The fundamental responsibility of the pollster is to seek out, understand, and to make apparent what that collective wisdom is all about.

In the last 12 months, Canadians have been faced with major issues, specifically free trade with the United States and the Meech

Lake Constitutional Accord, issues which have challenged their personal definitions of their country and their hopes and fears for their country. Soon they will be asked again to make choices and, through individual votes, to commit themselves to positions on these issues.

Tom Axworthy and I have been friends and colleagues for many years. We have worked together since the 1974 election campaign, where Tom worked on policy and I polled. Throughout the next decade we were constantly interacting — the policy-maker and the pollster.

This has been a difficult period for the Liberal party. During the last 15 years, Liberals did not question the values that had driven them forward. Those values have now been challenged within the party and within the party leadership. The Liberal party is now examining its roots, while at the same time looking ahead to its future. Both Tom and I are committed Liberals. We bring to the Liberal search for its "road to follow" a sense of uneasiness about the party and the relationship between its leadership and its traditional value system. We desire to help put the leadership back in touch with this value system.

It is to that end that we dedicate this book.

Martin Goldfarb
Toronto

PART ONE
LEADERSHIP AND CONVENTIONS

1

Tweedledum and Tweedledee?

Party is one of the most widely used and least understood terms in the political lexicon. What exactly is a political party? Edmund Burke gave the classic definition in 1770: "Party is a body of men promoting by their joint endeavours the national interest upon some particular principle in which they are all agreed."[1] Lest we get too rhapsodical, it is also wise to recall the definition attributed to Benjamin Disraeli: "Party is organized hypocrisy."

Burke's definition stresses principle; the great French liberal leader of the early nineteenth century, Benjamin Constant, similarly believed that "a party is a group of men professing the same political doctrine."[2] Doctrine, principle or shared opinion is the essence of the classic definition of party. This emphasis on common values or ideology was undoubtedly appropriate in the early formation of parliamentary parties, but is it accurate any longer to describe modern parties in the context of mass democracy as entities professing a set of consistent beliefs?

Unlike political parties in the era of Burke or of Constant, modern parties compete for the support of millions of citizens using technology that often reduces a political message to a mere 30 seconds. Are our parties simply vote-getting machines whose only purpose is to cobble together winning coalitions, or is there — beyond the competitive urge — a concept of society based on values?

Canadian parties are particularly prone to the criticism that pragmatism overrides belief. The overwhelming importance of religion and region in determining voter support in Canada has dismayed proponents of class-based politics and clear ideological choice alike.[3]

The dominant metaphor of party analysis in Canada comes from the market. Politicians are brokers and voters are buyers.

Party managers act as brokers between competing interests and regions, mediating conflict. Policy outcomes have little to do with ideology. Donald Smiley, one of Canada's eminent political scientists, expressed the academic consensus succinctly: "The two major parties do not differ profoundly in the social characteristics of their supporters, their orientation to public policy or how they are perceived by citizens."[4] Popular parlance reflects the scholarly view; Tweedledum and Tweedledee are slightly more sardonic expressions of the brokerage thesis.

If parties put a premium on winning and discount ideology, the basic questions remain: Who makes up the party? Who does the discounting?

A party is made up of three components: leader, activists and supporters. These three components interact, reinforce and reciprocally change one another. Any leader of a modern political party is in a commanding position. As the chief communicator of the party in an electronic age, the leader becomes the focus of the unrivaled attention. This single-minded concentration on personality gives a successful leader maximum leverage to define the agenda and prescribe the course. "The Presidency," said Theodore Roosevelt, "is a bully pulpit."

Pierre Trudeau, for example, persuaded the Liberal party to change its stand on cooperative federalism and, after years of effort, the country gradually came to accept this Liberal perspective on the Constitution. Joe Clark's personality, on the other hand, became the lightning rod for the numerous discontents in the Conservative party. In this case, the leader was blamed for deep-rooted maladies that went back generations.

Neither is leadership simply a case of Moses handing down the tablets. Leaders can change parties, but parties also change leaders. Every major Canadian party has a review mechanism that makes the leader ultimately accountable to the men and women who voluntarily fill the thousands of offices that make up the party organization. Twice in recent history — in 1966 against John Diefenbaker and in 1983 against Joe Clark — the Conservative party has used review mechanisms to dethrone the incumbent. In 1986 the Liberal party used its review mechanism to confirm John Turner as leader.

But the reciprocal relationship between the leader and the party cadre is normally far more subtle and diffuse than a straight-up vote for or against the holding of a leadership convention. The essence of the relationship is that a modern mass party is a *volunteer* organization. The number of Canadians interested in political activity is quite small. Two-thirds of Canadians vote, but only one-quarter discuss politics with friends and neighbors. Only 3% engage in party politics directly.[5]

The 3% of Canadians who volunteer for campaign duties and the few hundreds of thousands who take out membership cards in our three major federal parties are among the party activists who constitute the shock troops of Canadian political life. The apex of their involvement occurs at the leadership convention, one of the few remaining examples in the Western world of the old Greek ideal of direct democracy. The 3,000 Canadians who met in the Liberal convention in 1984, for example, were choosing not only a leader, but the next prime minister of Canada.

The nature of leadership commands much attention. As will be discerned presently, the dimensions of party support amongst the wider public is also a favorite topic of study. But the intervening variable, specifically the motivations, belief and impact of the party cadre, is much less appreciated. The data we collected at the 1983 and 1984 leadership conventions will give us some insight into the behavior of the politically motivated. A leadership convention puts the influence of party activists into stark relief — they are the ones choosing the man or woman who will "guide the destiny of millions." *But it is also the argument of this study that the values of this voluntary elite set the framework and define the agenda of the leaders they select.* The policy beliefs of the delegates who attended the conventions mattered.

The third component of a party is formed by the millions of durable partisans who make up its core support. An electorate is a constantly changing entity. New voters enter and others drop out. People often switch their vote and some even change their party. Within that sea of change, each party has a relatively stable band of people who readily identify themselves as Liberals, Conservatives or New Democrats and who retain this loyalty over time. Each party starts with this base and then reaches out to attract new voters, rekindle the interest of those who have dropped out or convert weak supporters in the ranks of the opposition. A popular political adage is "Ya dance with those that brung ya." Knowing the interests and concerns of one's stable coalition is the beginning of political wisdom. No party can hope to be successful by concentrating exclusively on the needs of its basic coalition (the band is too narrow), but taking one's core support for granted is an error of major proportions.[6]

What then is a political party? A political party is a voluntary association, made up of a leader, a cadre of activists and a committed body of support, who are drawn together by common beliefs or interests, and who are dedicated to influencing opinion.

By examining three climactic events — the Conservative convention of 1983, and the Liberal conventions of 1984 and 1986 — the relationships between leader, cadre, and coalition will become clear. Our special focus will be the activists — the voting delegates — because their role and influence is less appreciated than the two other well-known aspects of party.

CHOOSING A LEADER

Parties do many things. They set the political agenda, articulate concerns, organize governments, influence public policy and educate the public, but their most important task is to recruit the country's political leadership.[7]

Canada has invented an interesting way of choosing leaders. Like many of our institutions, the Canadian leadership convention is a hybrid of American practice and British tradition. The result, however, is something quite unique.[8]

In 1832 the Democratic party of the United States inaugurated the era of the open political convention by nominating Andrew Jackson as their standard-bearer. Party officials from around the country, rather than the party's elected representatives in Congress, became the center of decision making. Party activists claimed a right alongside the congressional leadership in deciding the party's nominee, thus broadening and enormously complicating the processes governing the quest for the presidency.

In Canada, the concept of the convention was introduced by the Liberal party. Prior to Confederation, in 1859 the Clear Grits held an important reform convention with 600 delegates. In 1893, the

Liberals under Laurier held a major policy conference, and in 1919, the Liberal party called Canada's first leadership convention, with 1,200 delegates in attendance. Then, Mackenzie King defeated William Fielding by 38 votes on the third ballot.

British tradition, however, was not completely ignored. Leaders in Britain were chosen by the parliamentary caucus (a practice not abandoned until the mid-1960s). While adopting the American invention of an extra-parliamentary mass convention, Canadian parties retained the more restrained British practice of a secret ballot. In Canada there would be no vulgar displays of "Manitoba, the great keystone province, votes all of its 23 delegates for William Lyon Mackenzie King."

The secret ballot changes the dynamics of Canadian conventions. Party notables can hope that their eminence will sway the choice of other delegates. Candidates can meet feverishly to make deals, but the truth is, no one knows how the individual delegate will behave in the privacy of the voting booth. Unlike American conventions, where the private commitments are publicly expressed, Canadian conventions contain an element of uncertainty about the vote totals. Delegates have to be wooed individually.

Survey research, therefore, is the best method of determining delegate attitudes and probable voting behavior. The three samples taken by Goldfarb Consultants prior to the conventions are not infallible. Obviously, the impact of the convention itself is absent from the calculations. But the pre-convention samples have been quite accurate in predicting the eventual outcomes.[9]

What is interesting is that in all three conventions the convention activity itself had little impact upon the voting intentions of the delegates. In these conventions, the delegates' minds were made up about whom to vote for before the convention even started, otherwise our projection technique never would have worked.

The data collected on delegate attitudes and voting behavior prior to the Conservative and Liberal conventions not only proved to be reliable in predicting the outcome of both conventions, but also provided a rich tableau of the motivations and beliefs of the delegates.

THE ARGUMENT

Two principal arguments are made. First, the core values of the two major parties are now radically different. While each party has a powerful and pragmatic urge to win power — and this motivation conditions strategy and tactics — the activists of the two parties hold fundamentally contrasting positions about the direction that Canada should take.

Our two major parties have, in fact, reversed positions. The Conservative hero was Sir John A. Macdonald. Macdonald Conservatives believed in a strong central power, activist government and the vigorous protection of Canadian independence from the United States. The Liberal hero was Sir Wilfrid Laurier. Laurier Liberals believed in provincial autonomy, were suspicious of the state and advocated greater integration with the American giant. Yet, by the mid-1980s, the Liberal party had become the defender of the Macdonald national policy and the Conservatives now expressed Laurier's "sunny ways" with the provinces and the Americans.

This chasm between the two parties is of recent origin. In the mid-1960s, there were relatively few policy differences between the parties. Since that time, however, the two parties have traveled down opposite roads. We see evidence of this movement toward changing value positions poignantly reflected in the Meech Lake Accord and free-trade issues. This divergence is having a profound and important effect on Canadian politics.

Yet, the second major finding revealed by the data moderates the impact of the first. Party members are activists, not ideologues. They value winning and, as a result, their diverse positions become muted. The outcome of elections, therefore, does not reflect the true underlying values of the parties.

The brokerage theory of Canadian politics is confirmed by the emphasis both Conservative and Liberal delegates placed on winning. The data will demonstrate that, although the policy views of the candidates were important considerations for the delegates, the desire to win was uppermost.

As a result of this drive to win, neither the press nor the public perceive the very real differences between the parties. The street view of Tweedledum and Tweedledee — the view that the two parties are essentially the same — is not accurate, but it results because of both parties' vacillations between brokerage politics and policy.

The brokerage maneuvers are hardly surprising. Delegates to Conservative and Liberal conventions play for high stakes. Delegates supporting the eventual victors in each convention — Brian Mulroney and John Turner — placed the highest premium on the electability of their candidates; policy views were secondary. Mulroney's views were moderate, and many of his supporters were from the far right, but for the delegates, the most important ingredient was the fact that he was perceived to be the best man to beat the dreaded Grits. John Turner was viewed as being on the conservative extreme of the Liberal party and many of his delegates saw themselves as more centralist than their candidate. He too, however, was viewed as a winner.

John Turner, in particular, finds it difficult to lead his party because he faces a different party now than the one he first came to know in the 1950s. He was elected, however, because his party desperately wanted to win. Liberals today want power as much as their predecessors, but now they want to use that power for an interventionist agenda. Parties may put their values on hold while they prepare a pragmatic program to win power, but if they acted on their true beliefs, no one would be likely to confuse a Liberal with a Conservative.

Turner compromised to gain power but, on the eve of an election, the specter of Liberal values is returning to haunt him. In 1984, the Liberal conscience wrestled between policy and the desire to win. Brokerage politics won the debate. Again in 1987, the issue of Meech Lake confronted head-on the policy convictions of most Liberals. By not opposing the Accord — because of fears of a Quebec backlash — the party leadership again opted for winning. This might be successful short-term politics, but it created confusion in the public mind about where the Liberal party stood and now stands, a problem that has persistently haunted Turner's leadership. He and his party have been wrestling one with the other; their debate is not yet over.

Before turning to the conventions and an explicit treatment of our argument, we should first explain the political context of the 1983 and 1984 conventions. We must begin with the Liberal ascendancy.

2

The Liberal Ascendancy:
1935-1984

Numbers, the stock and trade of the polling profession, give politics an exactness and permanence that is almost wholly absent from the subject matter itself. Analyzing election returns seems to be completely straightforward. A party's percentage goes up or down, and by sampling one can discover whether a trend is uniform or confined to particular regions or segments of the population.

This concreteness masks as much as it reveals, however. No election is ever static. Electoral majorities are majorities of the moment. V. O. Key, the Harvard pioneer in election studies, captures this reality best: "No sooner has a popular majority been constructed than it begins to crumble."[1]

Generations pass away; new ones spring up to take their place. Individuals decide to vote or stay at home. Most Canadians identify with one party or another, but often they switch their vote and, occasionally, they change their allegiance. Above all, Canadians react to the world around them. When values change, social conditions evolve or the economy grows or shrinks, peoples' hopes, dreams and fears are altered. Individuals change, partially in response to external events, as they make their passage through life. Expectations for education meld into hopes for a job, which become dreams for a house, which evolve into concerns about schools and are finally transferred into interest in health care and pensions. The electorate is in a state of constant change and constant volatility.

Parties must be alert to these changing patterns and be prepared to adapt. For most citizens, identification with a party is fragile. Party support is part of the socialization process; one is influenced by family, friends and community surroundings. According to one study, for example, six out of ten Liberal supporters had fathers who supported the Liberal party.[2]

Traditional ties, however, can be overcome easily by events. Whether attachment to party begins as an inherited family trait or as the result of conscious choice, there is a continuous process of either reinforcement or disintegration. Short-term forces such as the personality of a leader, the party's stand on a given issue or the general performance of a government can strengthen a person's identification or move a weak supporter to a strong partisan or an active participant. These same factors also could turn a supporter into an abstainer or a switcher. If the tide is heavy enough, they may even compel him to change party identification itself.[3]

Aware of the volatility of the voter, parties work to maintain the inheritance passed down by preceding generations of partisans. Maintaining the base is a pre-condition for political success. Parties recruit the non-aligned and those just entering the electorate. Immigrants and young people constantly replenish the voting pool. Parties also attempt to convert the supporters of the opposition. Voting shifts, though, are usually small. Most elections do not seem to show much movement. But behind this surface stability is a sea of change. People move to parties, away from parties, into the voting pool or out of the electorate. The permanence of an electoral pattern consists not in the perfect correspondence of children's loyalties with those of their parents, but in the stability of the flow between parties.

From 1935 to 1984, the Liberal party of Canada was the acknowledged master of this process of reinforcement, conversion and adaptation. It maintained its historic base, it moved skillfully in tandem with changing social and economic realities and it continually replenished itself by attracting handsome support from immigrants and youthful voters.

This half century of dominance provides the background for the leadership politics of 1983-84. The Conservatives were desperate to break the Liberal hold. The Liberals had to discover once more the secret for keeping up with the times. To understand the dilemma faced by our parties in the 1980s, one must begin with the politics of 1935.

SIX PARTY ERAS

Every election is about change, and any party system is in constant flux, though the magnitude of change varies greatly. Hundreds of thousands of people alter their voting pattern every election, but if the flow between the parties is consistent with past voting (i.e., if the end result is about the same), the outcomes are classified as **maintaining** elections. However, voters sometimes change their normal allegiance, and then return to their traditional base. This gives us a **deviating** election. Occasionally the transformations are profound and lasting; a realignment has taken place. These are the **critical** elections.[4]

Realignment comes gradually if the groups or regions that strongly support a party change their size as a proportion of the total electorate. Canadian farmers, for example, strongly favor the Conservative party, but farmers have declined dramatically as a percentage of the work force, thus reducing Conservative prospects. In the United States, the shift of the population to the Sun Belt and away from the industrial Northeast has aided the fortunes of the Republican party.

Realignment can come more dramatically in response to sweeping events or to the emergence of dominant personalities. The Depression shattered the reputation of the Conservative party and caused such distress that two new parties, the Social Credit party and the Cooperative Commonwealth Federation (CCF), were created in the upheaval.

Parties are not mere bystanders to these events. They can respond vigorously and make the social dynamics work for them, as Franklin Roosevelt's creation of the New Deal coalition demonstrated. They can even force the pace of change themselves. The Liberal party's gamble in choosing the French-Canadian Catholic Wilfrid Laurier as party leader in an age of religious intolerance and racial prejudice transformed Canadian politics in one bold stroke.

There have been six distinct party eras in Canadian history.[5] The first, Sir John A. Macdonald's Conservative constellation around the National Policy, lasted until 1896. Macdonald's alliance of Tory Loyalists, Montreal business interests intents and *ultramontane* French-Canadian *Bleus* swept six of Canada's first seven elections and only lost in 1874 because of the Pacific scandal.[6]

In 1887, the Liberal party chose Laurier as leader, and in 1896 Laurier took Quebec away from the Conservative party. In the critical election of 1896, the Liberals took 53% of the vote in Quebec, increasing their seats from 37 to 49. With 48% of the vote, a decline of 5% since 1891, the Conservatives won only 16 seats in Quebec (a drop of 12 seats from the previous election). In the rest of Canada, the results were 72 Conservatives, 69 Liberals, and 7 independents, making the Quebec switch the central factor in Laurier's victory. If the 1896 election was the breakthrough, the election of 1900 was the consolidation. The Liberals took 87% of the seats in Quebec, 51% of the vote across the country and won by 133 seats to 80.

Laurier's success in using his 1896 breakthrough to alter voting behavior permanently was the best indicator of his prowess as a politician. Elections can be won because of a particular congruence of special factors, but can the time in power be used to make the gains hold up? In this respect, the 1900 election was even more significant than that of 1896.[7]

The 1896/1917 two-party system came to an end in the wartime election of 1917, and Canadian politics remained in transition until 1935. World War I had split the Liberal party, and its aftermath had led to the Winnipeg general strike, the Progressive party movement and even a farmers' government in Ontario. A three-party system emerged in 1921 when Mackenzie King, the new leader of the Liberal party, formed a minority government with 116 seats, compared with 64 for the Progressives and 50 for the Conservatives. Regionalism fragmented the vote. The Progressives took the Prairies, the Conservatives Ontario, and the Liberals Quebec and the Maritimes. By the 1926 election, the Progressives had declined decisively to third-party status, receiving only 5.3% of the vote and Canada seemed to be veering again to a two-party system. King's Liberals won 46% of the vote, compared to 45% for the Conservatives. In 1930, R. B. Bennett's Conservatives turned the tables by winning a majority government, with 49% of the vote to King's 45%. In this era, the two major parties were fiercely competitive, with narrow swings of 1 or 2% deciding the government.

THE KING COALITION

The Depression permanently shattered Canada's two-party system, dealt a mortal blow to Conservative prospects for two decades and created the underlying conditions that were responsible for nearly 50 years of Liberal dominance.

The Liberal party governed Canada for 42 of the 49 years between 1935 and 1984. Franklin Roosevelt's successive victories in 1932 and 1936 established the New Deal coalition. Mackenzie King's successive triumphs in 1935 and 1940 created the base for a Liberal coalition that made his party the most successful political organization in the Western democracies.

Until 1935, the Conservative and Liberal parties had been nearly equal in strength. Macdonald had dominated the first era of Canadian politics, Laurier the second, and there had been a stand-off in the third. In a 1965 national election survey, for example, the two parties engaged equal support among Canadians who had entered the electorate before 1911: 34% of the 1911 cohort supported the Liberal party, 35.9% the Conservatives. For Canadians who entered the electorate during the 1930s, however, the percentages were dramatically altered: 39.9% supported the Liberal party and only 24.6% favored the Conservatives.[8] Compared to their parents, the generations that came of voting age in the 1930s and 1940s were 10 to 15% more inclined to support the Liberal party. Mackenzie King's skillful political response to traumatic events, such as the Depression and World War II, gave his party the lead, and henceforth, a preference would be passed on through family socialization. The Liberal party broke out of the pack between 1935 and 1940. King's successors would merely have to maintain the status quo and they would be victorious.

Building on Laurier's foundation of francophone support, King secured the support of a newly industrialized Canada by introducing social security and Keynesian economics. The Liberal party acquired the reputation of being both a sound manager and a party with a social conscience. Following World War II, the Liberal government also championed large-scale immigration, as Laurier had done, and the party reaped the benefits of this replenishment.

Regionally, King built a party that elected members from all parts of the country. In this regard, he was aided by Canada's four-party system. The Liberal party had not been strong in the West since the days of Laurier, but the two new parties formed in the 1930s, the CCF and Social Credit, both sprang from the same Prairie soil. In a four-party system, the Liberals could elect members from Western Canada with only a little more than 30% of the vote.

The Depression decimated the Conservatives, the Liberal party's only rival for office, and the fractured party system split the opposition vote among three contenders. Laurier's Quebec base was kept secure and the party's newly discovered social policies won moderate support across the spectrum. Mackenzie King had put together a classic center coalition.

THE DIEFENBAKER REALIGNMENT

The 1957 election was the greatest upset in Canadian electoral history, and John Diefenbaker's 1958 victory was the most massive. Showing the ravages of being in power for 22 years, the Liberal party and its 76-year-old leader, Louis St. Laurent, could not compete with the charismatic Prairie politician. Diefenbaker's 1957 victory originated in Western Canada where he won 21 seats, compared to nine for the Conservatives in 1953. In 1958, he made a Conservative dream come true by winning 50 seats in Quebec; the Liberal party's new leader, Lester B. Pearson, won only 25 in the party's traditional base. The 1958 election saw also the decline of the third and fourth parties, with the CCF losing 17 seats and the Social Credit 19.

Diefenbaker could not consolidate his 1958 victory into a widescale realignment as Laurier had done in 1900, or King in 1940. He did, however, secure a partial realignment by making the Conservative party a dominant force in the Prairies.[9]

The focus of power in the Conservative party now shifted from Ontario to the West. In 1953, the Conservatives had won 33 seats in Ontario and only 18 outside the province. During Diefenbaker's tenure as leader, the Conservative party in six elections won 63% of the seats in Western Canada. But as the Conservatives prospered in the West, they suffered in Ontario. Under Laurier and King, the Liberals had strength in the old Clear-Grit fiefdom of

Western Ontario, though Toronto was never central to Liberal strategies. Under Lester Pearson it became so. Suffering one of the worst defeats in Canadian history in 1958, Pearson built his party back up from the depths. In 1963, the Liberals received 41.7% of the vote to the Conservatives' 32.8%. The two minor parties received sufficient votes to prevent the re-emergence of the two-party system, but nowhere near enough to be perceived as major parties.

Diefenbaker increased his party's standing in the West, Pearson made Ontario vital to the Liberal coalition, and regionally based third parties became permanent fixtures of the Canadian scene. The pattern of Canadian politics had been set for the next 20 years.

THE TRUDEAU ERA

At first glance, the designation of the Trudeau era as a sixth distinct phase in the evolution of the Canadian party system seems somewhat overblown. True, the Liberal party under Pierre Trudeau continued its string of successes, winning four out of five elections and governing Canada from 1968 to 1984, save for only the nine-month Joe Clark regime from 1979 to 1980. But Trudeau's winning formula did not differ in its essentials from the framework established by his predecessors.

With some slight variations, he built on the francophone base delivered by Laurier, the centrist support across class lines that was the legacy of King, and the stark regional dimensions that were the product of the Diefenbaker-Pearson partial realignment. Elections after 1962–1963 were more maintaining campaigns than critical contests like those of 1896 or 1935.

The components of the modern Liberal coalition are diverse. The party overall enjoys strong support from Roman Catholics, francophones and a significant plurality of young people, big-city dwellers and ethnic Canadians.[10] The Conservative party usually leads the Liberal party among English-Canadians, Protestants, those living in small towns and farmers. Traditionally, the New Democratic Party is not ahead of the major parties in any category, but it does better among men than women and organized labor than non-union families. Tables I, II and III, data collected from 1974 to 1982 by Goldfarb Consultants, demonstrate the areas of strength for each of the three parties.

TABLE I

For Which Party Would You Be Most Likely To Vote In The Next Federal Election?	% of Canadians who indicated "Liberal"			
	April 1974	June 1977	May 1978	March 1981
Total	49	58	45	43
Male	47	57	42	42
Female	50	58	49	43
Under 25	53	54	46	49
25-34	49	52	44	51
35 and over	48	63	45	45
BC	40	58	26	21
Prairies	30	39	30	22
Ontario	48	57	39	42
Quebec	65	73	70	70
Atlantic	40	53	46	35
Union	N/A	54	N/A	N/A
Ethnic	N/A	54	N/A	N/A

TABLE II

For Which Party Would You Be Most Likely To Vote In The Next Federal Election?	% of Canadians who indicated "Conservative"			
	April 1974	June 1977	May 1978	March 1981
Total	28	25	38	38
Male	32	24	41	37
Female	25	26	34	38
Under 25	22	24	34	29
25-34	20	27	37	26
35 and over	34	24	39	39
BC	30	23	50	51
Prairies	47	47	55	55
Ontario	29	24	40	36
Quebec	13	10	18	20
Atlantic	42	32	40	44
Union	N/A	22	N/A	N/A
Ethnic	N/A	31	N/A	N/A

TABLE III

For Which Party Would You Be Most Likely To Vote In The Next Federal Election?	% of Canadians who indicated "NDP"			
	April 1974	June 1977	May 1978	March 1981
Total	23	16	16	19
Male	21	17	15	21
Female	25	14	17	19
Under 25	25	21	19	22
25-34	31	19	17	23
35 and over	18	12	15	16
BC	30	19	23	28
Prairies	23	14	14	23
Ontario	23	19	21	22
Quebec	22	12	8	10
Atlantic	18	15	14	21
Union	N/A	24	N/A	N/A
Ethnic	N/A	15	N/A	N/A

The fact that the Liberal party under Pierre Trudeau maintained a winning coalition rather than dramatically altering a piece of Canadian politics in no way diminishes the accomplishment. Canada changed mightily from the mid-1960s to the mid-1980s, and the ability of the Liberal party to retain its major blocks of support was no mean feat.

The Trudeau era, however, merits consideration as a distinct party phase for three main reasons. First, Pierre Trudeau was able to win heavy support from young people in every election. Most of the baby-boom generation cast their first votes for the Liberal party.[11]

The baby-boom generation, a huge oversized cohort of people numbering more than six million Canadians, is the dominant demographic feature of our time. Prior to the baby boom, the average number of births in Canada was approximately 250,000 per year, but from 1951 to 1966, 400,000 to 500,000 births were recorded every year. Double the size of previous generations, the baby-boom generation drastically affected every aspect of society that it rolled through — baby food, schools, rock and roll, jobs and job training now, old-age homes and pensions tomorrow. The first baby-boomers voted in 1968; the last of this cohort voted in 1984. The baby-boomers grew up with Trudeau and most of them voted for him by margins of two to one.

The importance of Trudeau's appeal to first-time voters is demonstrated by the election of 1974, when, despite popular mythology about the impact of wage and price controls, the Liberals actually suffered a slight net loss of switchers. (They lost 9.8% of their 1972 vote to the other parties and only gained 8.1%.) But among the newly eligible in 1974, the Liberals won 45% and the Conservatives only 17%.[12] In the swing province of Ontario, 70% of the new vote went Liberal. Similarly, in 1979 a Conservative majority was prevented because new voters voted Liberal by a margin of three to two. King made the Depression generation a Liberal strength. Trudeau persuaded the largest generation in Canadian history to begin their political involvement by voting Liberal.

Trudeau inherited a four-party system in 1968; when he retired in 1984, it was down to three. The Social Credit party, centered in British Columbia, Alberta and Quebec, ceased to be an important factor in politics. In 1965, the Social Credit party won 17% of the vote in B.C., 23% in Alberta and 18% in Quebec. In 1980, the corresponding percentages were .1, 1 and 6.[13]

Right-wing and populist, Social Credit support in British Columbia and Alberta drifted to the Conservative party during the Trudeau era. Diefenbaker had made the Conservative party the most powerful force in the West. The coalescence of the right into one party made them into a colossus.

King had benefited from a four-party split in the West. The Liberals under Trudeau suffered when the parties were reduced to three. In Quebec, however, the decline of Social Credit worked in the opposite direction from the trends in the West. With the Liberal party already dominant in Quebec, Trudeau added to the base: from 46% of the support in 1965, to 53% in 1968, to 54% in 1974, to 62% in 1979 and finally, to 68% in 1980. Under Trudeau, the regional patterns bequeathed by the Diefenbaker-Pearson realignment were continued, but considerably sharpened. The Tories became stronger in the West, and the Liberals paramount in Quebec.

The third electoral dimension of the Trudeau era that commands attention is the change within the Liberal coalition. In many respects there was a continuity in the kinds of people who voted Liberal from the days of St. Laurent to Trudeau. Roman Catholics, for example, support the Liberal party in election after election. But in one key variable — socio-economic class — the Trudeau years exhibited a profound difference.

The Liberal party has always had good support from Canadians of all classes but traditionally it has been most attractive to upper-income Canadians. In 1968, for example, according to John Meisel's election study, the Liberal party received above-average support from those who placed themselves in the upper class but its proportion of the vote from lower-class identifiers was substantially below average.[14] Level of education, a good measure of socio-economic status, reflects the same trend: in 1968, 60% of the university-trained supported the Liberal party, compared to 46% of those with secondary education and 44% of those with only elementary schooling.

By 1980, this trend had been reversed. In that election, the highest percentage support for the Liberal party (46%) came from those with elementary education. Next were those with secondary education (44%) and last were the university-trained, with only 42% of those with higher education supporting the Liberal party. (See footnote 10, for a table on Liberal party support.) In the 1980s, those Canadians with the greatest fidelity to the Liberal party were those with low incomes — Canadians making under $20,000 a year. Weakest support was among the wealthy. Trudeau had welded young people, women and low-income Canadians much more firmly to the Liberal party than had been the case in the past, but he suffered a corresponding decline in traditional Liberal support among men, upper-income Canadians and residents of the West.

In the Trudeau era, political demarcations became more fixed. The Atlantic provinces were split along traditional lines, Quebec was solidly Liberal and the West was solidly Conservative. Francophones, minorities and low-income Canadians were firm in their allegiance to the Liberals, high-income Canadians became firm in their opposition. Elections turned on two swing factors — Ontario and middle-income Canadians.

This was the legacy inherited by the two major parties as they made their leadership decisions in 1983 and 1984. The Liberal party sought to keep the Trudeau coalition, which resembled the classic formulations of social-democratic parties, to lure back high-status Canadians who had departed and to break into the Conservative stronghold in the West.

The Conservative task was more daunting. They had to overcome the ingrained habits of most Canadian voters. Fifty years of Liberal dominance had given that party a two-to-one lead in partisan identification.[15] Quebec appeared to be more solidly Liberal than at any time since Laurier. But as the economy had turned sour, the expectations of the baby-boom generation who had cast their first votes for Trudeau were dashed. Volatility among Canadian voters increased. Both parties could make their choice buoyed with hope.

3

Anyone but Clark

Leadership choice is influenced, as in a general election, by a combination of short-term factors and long-term trends. The 3,006 accredited delegates to the Conservative convention in June 1983[1] faced one overwhelming and immediate issue — were they for or against the continued stewardship of Charles Joseph Clark, leader of the Conservative party since February 1976 and, from May 1979 to March 1980, sixteenth prime minister of Canada. Above all, the 1983 contest was a referendum on Joe Clark, a referendum that Clark lost. Martin Brian Mulroney, the eventual victor, knew his party well when he told a journalist days before the actual vote that "this party has made up its mind to dump Joe Clark. What it has not decided yet is who to replace him with."[2]

But if pro- or anti-Clark sentiment was the driving force of the convention, the views of delegates on this preeminent question were shaped by a variety of motivations. For some delegates, Clark was a pawn of the party establishment that had undermined the populist hero, John Diefenbaker. Nineteen eighty-three would simply be round four of a battle that had begun 20 years earlier. Ideology congealed with this factionalism to produce a potent challenge. Clark was a moderate trying to lead a party that had steadily drifted toward the right. By 1983, a clear majority of the delegates classified themselves as right of center and most of those ended up voting for Brian Mulroney. More fatally, Clark was found wanting on the critical dimension of "winnability." Desperate to break the Liberal ascendancy, delegates searched for a candidate and a formula that would guarantee electoral success. Brian Mulroney was perceived to be a winner. Joe Clark was not.

It was as simple as that.

POWER BLOCS

A leader does not have carte blanche within a party; he must contend with independent sources of influence. The first is the elected caucus. A leader must have the respect and the support of caucus. They are the leader's daily companions in the parliamentary wars; they exert an important impact on the party notables and the grass-roots activists. They are the primary sources of information for the media (and the media, in turn, shape public and party opinion about the leader), and by responding daily to events in the House of Commons, they have the predominant voice in party policy.

Leaders, of course, have great resources in dealing with caucus. Personal loyalties and friendships are formed in the crucible of parliamentary life. Appointment to the cabinet or a *shadow* cabinet in opposition are the prerogative of the leader. The image and strength of a leader can also be the prime ingredient in a member's personal victory.

Leaders of caucus, however, must be wooed; they cannot be commanded. Made up of elected politicians in their own right — with sources of support independent of the leadership — caucus is the one group to which a leader is accountable on a continuing basis.

Caucus no longer elects a leader. The Liberal caucus lost the formal power in 1919; the Conservative caucus in 1927. Because the Conservatives had won only 103 seats in 1980, the 103 Conservative members of Parliament and 22 senators were only a handful of votes out of the 3,006 accredited delegates to the June 1983 convention. Brian Mulroney was not even a member of the caucus when he was elected leader.

But if a caucus does not have the ability to choose a leader, it still has the power to depose one. A leader who has lost the support of his parliamentary peers will likely lose his legitimacy within the party as a whole. For the wider public, a leader who cannot even unite his own party gives little reassurance that he will be able to govern the nation.

Joe Clark lost his job because he lost the confidence of his caucus. Perhaps he had never gained it. Supported in 1976 by only a handful of his colleagues, Clark did not begin his leadership with a secure parliamentary base. Within a year, Jack Horner had bolted to the Liberals and Robert Coates, an avowed Clark opponent, had been elected president of the Conservative party. In 1979 the Conservative party won the election in spite of Joe Clark. His image as a weak leader was the most important factor in preventing a Conservative majority and members of caucus knew that they were not indebted to their leader for their own personal success. Because Clark was not in power long enough as prime minister to use the formidable powers of that office to build a caucus coalition, his defeat in February 1980 left him at the mercy of his caucus critics.

When one-third of the delegates at the 1981 Conservative convention voted for a leadership review, Clark had to promise his caucus that he would resign if his numbers did not improve. At the Winnipeg meeting in 1983, when he failed to improve on that percentage, Clark knew that he would face a caucus revolt if he did not live up to his earlier promise. A prominent Mulroney supporter in caucus, Elmer Mackay, had signed letters from 48 of his colleagues calling on Clark to resign. A clear majority of the caucus voted in favor of a leadership convention at the Winnipeg meeting.[3]

Clark's resignation after winning 66% of the support of the 2,400 delegates at the January 1983 Winnipeg meeting has always surprised observers. Why was two-thirds not enough? What is not understood is the fact that Canadian parliamentary parties are like a dual monarchy: one must command majority support both among the party activists and the caucus. Each has a veto; the party's right is enshrined in the Conservative constitution, while the caucus' power is informal but no less real.[4] At Winnipeg, the party activists had voted to support the leader, but the result was not impressive enough to sway the decision of the caucus. The caucus was in revolt. Clark knew it, and only a new leadership convention could clear the air.

THE EXTRA-PARLIAMENTARY PARTY

The fate of Joe Clark demonstrates that caucus support is crucial. The history of John Diefenbaker, however, offers another lesson — it is not enough only to have the support of caucus. The extra-parliamentary wing of the party must also be satisfied generally with the leadership or it will use the institutions it controls — the national executive and national conventions — to express its displeasure.

The rebellion between 1963 and 1966 of the extra-parliamentary wing of the Conservative party against the leadership of John Diefenbaker set in motion a series of conflicts and schisms that were still being played out at the 1983 convention.

In 1963, a Cabinet revolt against Prime Minister Diefenbaker failed when the caucus rallied to the leader. After the loss of the 1963 election, dissidents used the February 1964 meeting of the national association to raise the leadership issue again, and at various meetings throughout 1965 the executive of the party was a forum for the anti-Diefenbaker faction. In the fall of 1966, Dalton Camp, the president of the party, publicly called for a leadership review. That November, in the most bitter convention in Canadian political history, Camp's team prevailed by a narrow margin of 62 votes over the Diefenbaker loyalists. Of the 96 Conservative members of the House of Commons, 71 signed a petition requesting Diefenbaker to continue as leader, but a leadership convention was called for September 1967. A decisive moment in Canadian political history had occurred: leaders, henceforth, would be accountable both to their caucus and to the party activists.

From that moment on, the composition of national conventions — who attended, from what regions and in what manner — became a vital political ingredient. In the 1983 Conservative convention, the 3,006 accredited delegates were divided into three nearly-equal blocs. For the Conservatives, 1,115 delegates (or 37%) were senior riding delegates, 972 (or 32%) from riding and campus-club youth and 919 (or 31%) ex-officio or automatic delegates. This may be contrasted with the delegate composition at the 1984 Liberal convention, where a greater percentage (1,740 delegates or 51%) of the 3,442 delegation were senior riding delegates and a smaller proportion (762 delegates or 22%) were youth delegates; 27%, or 940 of the Liberal delegates, were ex officio or automatic.

When party activists speak enthusiastically about the "grassroots" they are usually referring to the delegates elected in riding meetings. But at the 1983 Conservative convention, senior riding delegates made up only 37% of the total. Even when the two youth delegates elected in each riding are included in the total, elected riding delegates comprised only 56% of the Tory delegates.

Grassroots usually implies, too, the notion that the riding delegates are comprised of the local executives, the president, secretary-treasurer, and so forth, who form the voluntary infrastructure of the party. This too can be deceiving. Approximately 40% of the Conservative and Liberal delegates ran as part of a slate.[5] Those slates were elected because of their loyalty to the candidate, not because of their fidelity to the local constituency organization.[6]

The convention delegates are selected by a strict criterion (six delegates per riding) and include as well a predetermined number of automatic appointments from the national executive. The one unknown in the Conservative and Liberal conventions was the number of youth delegates. Like other parts of the party constitution, a formula is set, but the number of clubs is open-ended. This produced one of the most remarkable aspects of the Conservative convention. A third of the delegates were young. In addition to the youth ex-officio delegates on the national executive and the two youth delegates elected per riding, nearly 400 youth delegates attended the Tory convention as representatives of post-secondary institutions. These 'post-secondary institutions' included hairdressing salons, hostels and the like. The Clark, Mulroney and Crosbie organizations simply created scores of instant clubs to elect three delegates each. In Newfoundland, for example, the Crosbie team organized 21 clubs to produce 63 delegates, almost as many delegates as the whole province had sent to the 1976 leadership convention (78 delegates in 1976 as compared with 171 in 1983). This huge youth bloc of 1983 was a new phenomenon in Conservative conventions.

The tradition of nearly one-third automatic or appointed delegates has a longer pedigree. In 1967, 46% of the delegates to that Conservative leadership convention were either ex officio or appointed by the convention organizing committee as delegates at large. This discretionary power of appointment by a central committee was later replaced by a provincial allocation formula with provincial executives having the power of appointment.

Two things stand out about ex-officio delegates in the Conservative party. The first is that a leader is able to appoint a significant number of his followers — party fundraisers, the campaign committee and policy advisory committees. Ex-officio delegates, in a word, are the party establishment. It is not surprising that Joe Clark received by far the largest amount of ex-officio support (45%) on the first ballot since he had appointed most of them.[7]

But just as significant as the built-in advantage for the leader is the provincial orientation of the Conservative ex-officio delegates. Many of the automatics are appointed by provincial authorities, not the central executive dominated by the leader's followers. Fully one-third of the 900 automatics in 1983 were provincial legislative members and nearly 200 additional delegates were appointed because of their provincial status. A Peter Lougheed influencing the Alberta legislative delegation or a Brian Mulroney winning control of the Quebec provincial party executive that, in turn, had the power to appoint 38 delegates at large, represents an important decentralization of national authority. This delegation to provincial executives within the party apparatus is a reflection of the powerful provincial Conservative parties that developed in the 1970s. In 1967, a central party committee appointed 23% of the total delegates at large. In 1983, these delegates at large were appointed by provincial parties.[8]

THE INS VERSUS THE OUTS

For 20 years, from 1963 through 1983, the four power blocs within the Conservative party were engaged in civil war. The atmosphere of distrust, the shifting alliances, the outbreaks of discord and the occasional full-scale combat between the leader, caucus, the party establishment and the grassroots activists became a preoccupation and an innate character trait of the Conservative party.

The initial dispute was clear enough — John Diefenbaker wanted to retain his job and Dalton Camp wanted to take it away — but after 20 years of strife, lines became blurred, new grievances had been piled upon the old, and the original cause of the fight was lost in a welter of ambition and rancor. An outsider, Brian Mulroney, a man not really aligned with either warring faction, finally emerged from the turmoil and succeeded in taking the ultimate prize. In the meantime, the Liberal party profited mightily by their opponent's disunity.

In 1956, John Diefenbaker, a westerner, a populist and a man descended from a German background in a country dominated by English and French-Canadian charter groups, won the leadership of the Conservative party on his third try after failing in 1942 and 1948. Diefenbaker shifted the focus of power within his party away from the Ontario party establishment and toward his new prairie base. By 1966, Diefenbaker's strength in the party reflected his support in the country. He was a hero to small-town rural Canada, but seemed almost comic, and certainly a relic from the past, to the rapidly growing urban centers of Montreal, Toronto and Vancouver.

In phase one of the Conservative civil war, the Diefenbaker faction, centered in caucus and drawing support from the new Western base, was outmaneuvered and eventually defeated by Dalton Camp, who drew his support from the party infrastructure, especially the student wing of the Conservative party. Joe Clark, then president of the Progressive Conservative Student Federation (reflecting the overwhelming sentiment of the college Conservatives) had called on Diefenbaker to resign in early 1965 and Clark later became an important ally of Camp's in the climactic November 1966 convention.

In 1967, Robert Stanfield, the premier of Nova Scotia and the candidate favored by Dalton Camp, defeated John Diefenbaker and seven other prominent Conservatives to become leader of the Conservative party. Stanfield was a moderate — progressive on social and linguistic policy and mildly conservative on economics. Ideology played little role in 1967; Stanfield's opponent on the last ballot was Duff Roblin, former premier of Manitoba and also a moderate. Regionalism, however, did play a part: many of Diefenbaker's followers went to Roblin because he was from the West. The urban moderates, however, now controlled the leadership. They had always been the dominant factor among the party notables or establishment, and the party activists had given the overwhelming percentage of the votes to progressive candidates.

Electoral success, however, was denied to Robert Stanfield. Beaten three times by Pierre Trudeau, Stanfield's position was constantly undermined by John Diefenbaker and his followers in caucus. The Conservative party continued to do well in the Prairies, Diefenbaker's legacy to his party, but Stanfield could not deliver the urban centers of modern Canada. Many in the caucus owed their election to Diefenbaker, not Stanfield. Sixteen members of the caucus defied Stanfield and stood with Diefenbaker in voting against the Official Languages Act in 1973, at a crucial time when the Liberals had only a minority government.

Ideology now began to congeal with personal bitterness to strengthen the sources of factionalism. Stanfield's advocacy of bilingualism and his support for a guaranteed annual income began to identify "Red Tories," or progressives, with those controlling the party's destiny. In his own time, Diefenbaker had been a progressive and he had led an activist government. By the early 1970s, many of his supporters were much stronger in their right-wing views — distrustful of the state and opposed to the welfare liberalism of the Trudeau government. Having lost control of the party in the 1960s, the Diefenbaker loyalists felt excluded and developed an "us" versus "them" mentality. This populist or anti-establishment faction now joined with an even larger group who were dissatisfied with the philosophical direction of the party.

It is important not to overemphasize the size of these factions. George Perlin, the Queen's University professor who has best analyzed modern Conservative politics, estimates that in 1976 the Diefenbaker faction made up only 15% of the delegates at the convention (albeit that 10 years is a long time to retain such loyalty) and that the right-wing ideological dissenters or pure non-interventionists made up 23% of the convention delegates.[9] In 1976, this populist-right-wing alliance once again took on the dominant establishment-centrist majority and once again lost. But this time they lost by only a narrow margin.

Nineteen seventy-six was phase three in the Conservative civil war. This time ideological and populist lines were more clearly drawn than in 1967. Jack Horner ran as the candidate of the Diefenbaker loyalists. Claude Wagner, Paul Hellyer and Sinclair Stevens were clearly identified as candidates of the right. Flora Macdonald, Brian Mulroney, John Fraser and Joe Clark were moderates identified with the Stanfield wing of the party. On the fourth ballot, Horner, Hellyer and Diefenbaker supported Claude Wagner. Macdonald, Fraser and the vast bulk of Brian Mulroney's delegates supported Clark (although Mulroney himself preferred not to indicate a choice).[10] Only Sinclair Stevens made a tactical move that defied ideological exactness in moving to Joe

Clark. Clark won by 65 votes on the fourth ballot, about the same margin that had sustained Dalton Camp in his victory as party president in 1966.

Between 1976 and 1983, Joe Clark and Brian Mulroney reversed roles. In 1976, Joe Clark succeeded because he was able to escape identification with the various cleavages that so divided the Conservative party. To put it succinctly, he was not a target of any of the factions until it was too late to stop him. Because his candidacy was not taken seriously until the very end of the campaign, he avoided the scrutiny that hurt the two top contenders, Claude Wagner and Brian Mulroney. With his strong regional base in Quebec, Wagner was always a strong candidate of the right. Early on, he became the man the moderates knew they must stop.

Brian Mulroney allowed himself to become the *bête noire* of the populist and right-wing offensive. Mulroney's candidacy did not have a strong policy component, although he was identified as a Stanfield Conservative. What he did have was support, concentrated in Montreal and Toronto, an urban, sophisticated style with obvious ties to the business establishment and the temerity to run for leader without having a seat in the House of Commons. The populist right succeeded in stopping the high-profile Mulroney, but in doing so they ignored Joe Clark who was thus able to emerge as the moderate alternative to Wagner. The moderate wing still had enough support to eke out one more victory. Brian Mulroney learned his lesson: in 1983, Joe Clark would be the target of the populist right and Mulroney would be careful in drawing attention.[11]

In 1976, approximately 25% of the Conservative party, as measured among delegates at that convention, formed a dissenting wing opposed to the dominant party establishment. By the 1980s, this dissenting wing had grown to include the 33% who cast their ballots against Joe Clark — in Ottawa in 1981 and in Winnipeg in 1983. Caucus agitation against Clark has already been described. The right-wing core which had bedeviled the career of Robert Stanfield continued to hinder Clark and, after the 1980 defeat, he lost even a majority following in caucus.

By and large, Clark continued to hold the support of the party notables or the establishment who made up nearly a third of the voting delegates in 1983. Clark's closest political confidante and campaign manager, Lowell Murray, put in place an effective organization that dominated most of the key party posts. But this very strength masked a weakness. The moderate wing had been in control of the party infrastructure since 1966. Individuals changed, but the overall orientation did not.

Gradually, among the activists of the party, resentment grew about the party establishment. In the Stanfield era, supporters of Diefenbaker unsuccessfully had sought the party presidency but moderates, like Frank Moores and Michael Meighen, had beaten back the challenge. But in 1977, Robert Coates won the party presidency and, increasingly, the populist right was able to make use of the elected positions on the national executive to harass the appointed campaign structure of the leader. In 1976, Perlin found that those most on the right considered themselves the furthest from the national elite.[12] By 1983, more than 60% of the delegates believed there was a party establishment, but only 19% considered themselves close to it.[13] In the 20-year Conservative civil war, populist sentiment gradually merged with right-wing belief. As the right grew in strength, the moderate establishment gradually became more beseiged. In 1983, phase four would see the populists dethroning the leader of the establishment wing as efficiently as the establishment had once downed a populist hero in 1966.

THE RIGHT-WING SURGE

The Conservative party is a brokerage party; it places a premium on winning. When Joe Clark failed to pass muster on this score, it was his most significant deficiency. In preparing for elections, Conservative strategists, for example, are level-headed and carefully assess how much radical change Canadians are prepared to accept. Conservative-party platforms bear little resemblance to the straight-forward right-wing appeals of Margaret Thatcher or Ronald Reagan. But when they feel from the heart rather than think from the head, the grassroots activists of the Conservative party are unabashedly right wing.

This ideological journey of the Conservative party from the centrist consensus of the Stanfield era to the right-wing militancy of the mid-1980s is one of the most dramatic changes in Canadian political history. It duplicates the passage of the Republican party from the middle-of-the-road Eisenhower era to the total dominance of the Reagan right. Whether this conversion will have as much of an impact on Canadian public policy as the Reagan revolution has had in the United States will depend on the evolution of Canadian values. Canada is not yet a clone of the United States, but the activist base of the Conservative party is close to being a clone of the Republican right.

As Chapter 5 will demonstrate, there were significant policy differences between Conservative and Liberal positions even in the mid-1960s, but what is truly remarkable is how much the Conservative party has changed since that era. Whether one measures changes over time on policy issues or ideological self-identification, there has been a rightward march.

Since 1967 the Conservative party has steadily become more anti-statist, more decentralist, increasingly pro-American and tougher on social-agenda issues such as abortion. The tables which follow show this progression of policy views since 1967.[14]

Approval of Policy Positions

Conservative Delegates 1967 and 1976	1967	1976
1. Provincial governments should have more power	32	63
2. Federal government should give more money to the provinces	55	71
3. Old age pension and baby bonus should only be paid to people who need them	66	88
4. Government ought to interfere less with business	61	77
5. Canadians' right to strike should not be restricted	23	19
6. Canada should take steps to bring its foreign policy more closely in line with that of the United States	20	32

Approval of Policy Positions

Conservative Delegates 1976 and 1983	1976	1983
1. Decreased trade barriers and free trade with the United States	65	77
2. Approval of capital punishment	64	80
3. Approval of abortion	61	36
4. Promote bilingualism	30	25

In 1967, 32% of delegates agreed with the policy position stating that provincial governments should have more power. In 1976, 63% agreed. In 1967, 66% supported a means test for old-age pensions and baby bonuses; by 1976 this had risen to 88%. Similarly, in 1976, 65% approved free trade, but by 1983, 77% of the delegates approved. In that seven-year period, support of capital punishment rose from 64% to 80%, while support declined for abortion.

In 1967, 59% of the Conservative delegates thought Canada should spend less on defense; in 1983, 72% thought Canada should spend more. In 1967, 58% of the Conservative partisans wanted special laws to regulate U.S. foreign investment; in 1983, 67% wanted to decrease the powers of the Foreign Investment Review Agency. In 1967, only 33% of Conservative delegates wanted more power for provincial governments, but by 1983 this had grown to 54%.

Three factors explain this ideological shift. First, in opposing the state and favoring the market, Canadian Conservatives were reacting to the economic difficulties that had plagued the Western world for a decade. Liberals or social democrats, such as Pierre Trudeau, James Callaghan, Jimmy Carter and Helmut Schmidt, were all in office when the dismal economic tides of the 1970s began to lash at their societies. Liberalism's solutions were found wanting. If active government did not work, perhaps less government was the solution.

In Canada, this general stance was reinforced by some specific policies of the Trudeau government. In creating Petro Canada, a state-owned oil company, the Liberals had built a symbol that drove the Alberta oil industry and their Conservative supporters into a frenzy. So, too, with decentralization. The Conservative support for provincial powers reflected the fact that the Liberals were the national government and Conservatives ran most of the provinces. Finally, Tory identification with the United States had much to do with the success of Ronald Reagan. In 1967, when only 19% of the delegates wanted a foreign policy more aligned with the Americans, the United States was fighting an unpopular war in Vietnam. In 1983, when 60% of the Tories favored President Reagan's tough line toward the Soviets, a conservative was in the White House, and the United States was tall in the saddle.

The shift in policy stance is also evident in ideological self-identification. Conservative partisans who identified themselves as being to the right of their party made up nearly 60% of the delegates in 1983. Red Tories, those favoring moving the party to the left, were a miniscule 4%. The ideological right had grown dramatically since 1976 and that growth spelt trouble for Joe Clark.[15]

Self-Identification of Conservative Delegates

	1976 Leadership Convention	May 1982 Policy Conference	1983 Leadership Convention
Identity with left	19	12	4
Identity with right	42	31	57

In 1976, the Republican right narrowly failed in its attempt to dislodge Gerald Ford and nominate Ronald Reagan and, also in 1976, the Conservative right narrowly failed in its attempt to elect Claude Wagner. The right was the largest bloc at the convention and a majority of its members voted for the Quebecker on the fourth ballot. But Clark received support from 79% of those identifying with the left and 72% of those identifying with the center and that was enough.[16] By 1980, however, the Republican right nominated Ronald Reagan and, in 1983, the Conservative right elected Brian Mulroney. In 1983, 57% of the delegates identified with the right and 75% of those supported Mulroney on the last ballot.[17] Clark again obtained 70% of the votes of the left and 62% of the votes of the center, but this time there were simply not enough moderates to stem the tide.

CHOOSING THE LEADER

On June 11, 1983, on the fourth ballot, the Progressive Conservative party chose Brian Mulroney to be its new leader over Joe Clark by a margin of 1,584 to 1,325. This time Clark was the issue. Mulroney won not because he was perceived to be the best leader (on most issues he ranked third in comparison to Clark and John Crosbie), but because he was regarded as the strongest alternative to Clark. He won, as the following table demonstrates, because he was not Joe.[18]

Rating of Candidates

	Clark	Mulroney	Crosbie
1. Ability to beat the Liberals if John Turner was leader	32	33	20
2. Least comfortable with as prime minister	17	15	4
3. Best represents Canada internationally	29	23	29
4. Best deals with Canada-U.S. relations	31	23	30
5. Trust least	15	26	3
6. Best for Canadian unity	39	30	15
7. Average impression rating (maximum 10)	6.4	6.2	6.8
8. Unimpressed	19	20	10
9. Very impressed	43	38	43

Clark's inability to dominate his caucus was the single most important factor precipitating the leadership review. The populist versus establishment tradition in the party ensured the existence of a large dissident group. The explosion of right-wing sentiment in the Conservative party put Clark at a disadvantage because he was the acknowledged leader of the moderate wing. But the final factor in sealing his fate was the perception that Clark could not win. In making their leadership choice, the Conservative delegates placed a premium on winning. Asked to rank the relative importance of issues against winnability, delegates gave the edge to winnability. Mulroney's supporters more than Clark's, in fact, opted for winning.[19]

In your selection of a candidate in the forthcoming convention, of ten points, how many would you place on his stand on particular issues and how many on his likelihood to beat the Liberals?	Importance Score (Average)		
	Total Delegates	Clark Supporters	Mulroney Supporters
Stand on issues	5.0	5.1	4.7
Ability to beat the Liberals	5.3	5.2	5.5

On this essential winnability factor, Mulroney had a clear edge over Clark among those delegates who were up for grabs after the field had been narrowed to Clark, Crosbie and Mulroney. They favored Mulroney over Clark by a margin of more than two to one as the candidate most likely to beat either John Turner or Pierre Trudeau.[20]

Rating of Candidates among delegates who supported a candidate other than Clark/Mulroney/Crosbie

	Clark	Mulroney	Crosbie
1. Ability to beat the Liberals if John Turner was leader	7	28	14
2. Ability to beat the Liberals if Pierre Trudeau was leader	11	24	11

Animosity to Joe Clark was one dynamic fueling the convention. Loyalty to him was the other. Clark's first ballot total of 1,091 was within striking distance of success. He was the only candidate with significant support in every region[21] (including Quebec where he virtually tied Brian Mulroney), he was the only moderate candidate with even a chance of stopping the challenge from the right wing, and he had a strong base of 45% among the nearly one-third of the delegates who were ex officio. His problem was that having achieved the 1,000-plus plateau, he had almost no second-ballot strength. He had squeezed out all the support he was going to get. It was not like 1976. No one walked to his box on the long afternoon of June 11, 1983.

But what support he did have stayed loyal, and this factor was important to the convention's final outcome. On the first three ballots, when it became obvious that Clark had no room to grow, he lost only 33 votes. There was no hemorrhaging of his support away from him. If Clark's support had been soft and had dissipated after the first ballot, John Crosbie might have gained enough votes to overtake Mulroney or, one of the third-tier candidates, Michael Wilson perhaps, might have emerged from the pack as Joe Clark had done in 1976. But this was not to be. Clark's supporters had fought beside him in the 1979 and 1980 national election campaigns. They had fought the review battles of 1981 and 1983. They would not desert him now. But they simply couldn't grow.

Brian Mulroney's 874 votes on the first ballot made him a strong second to Clark and the natural leader of the anti-Clark coalition. Thus it proved when Michael Wilson and Peter Pocklington moved to Mulroney's box after the first ballot.[22] His Quebec base gave him a solid foundation of between 350 and 400 votes. To that, he added 200 votes from Ontario, most of them representing youth clubs and a respectable showing of 13% of the ex officios. The smallest element of Mulroney's initial support (about 100 votes) came from elected English-speaking riding delegates,[23] the group that forms the core of the Conservative party.

Mulroney had many negatives working against him in 1983, but unlike 1976, he skillfully minimized the damage and maximized the opportunities. Trust was the factor that hurt him most — 26% of the delegates trusted him least — and his credibility was not enhanced when he publicly endorsed Joe Clark in December 1982 at the same time that his supporters were working frantically to send anti-Clark delegates to the Winnipeg review meeting. The anyone-but-Mulroney factor, in fact, was almost as large as the anyone-but-Clark. The crucial difference was that the anti-Mulroney delegates were heavily concentrated among Clark supporters while anti-Clark delegates were spread widely among the various candidates. Mulroney had room to grow. Clark had none.[24]

Would Not Vote For Clark/Mulroney Under Any Circumstances	Conservative Delegates, 1983	
	Clark	Mulroney
Total	26	25
Region		
West	23	39
Ontario	34	26
Quebec	21	20
Atlantic	19	24
Support Orientation		
Clark Delegates	–	48
Mulroney Delegates	46	–
Crosbie Delegates	45	22
Wilson Delegates	31	25
Crombie Delegates	15	32
Pocklington Delegates	52	12

Mulroney overcame his deficiencies by: 1) making Clark the target, not himself; 2) his organizational prowess in Quebec and in youth clubs; 3) his skill in appropriating the majority right-wing sentiment; 4) emphasizing his francophone background and the hope that he represented for a breakthrough in Quebec; and 5) emphasizing his ability to win, the central factor on the minds of most delegates. Mulroney ran a frugal campaign, concentrating on the delegates rather than on the media. This helped prevent him from becoming a focus of resentment. His youth organization saved the day in Quebec and won him his support in Ontario. Clark had stolen a march on Mulroney by organizing many early delegate meetings in Quebec. Nearly one-half of Mulroney's first ballot support came from Quebec, and one-half of that support came from youth delegates. Another quarter of his support came from Anglo youth, especially from Ontario.

Fully 46% of Mulroney's support on the first ballot came from youth delegates. In the showdown with Clark on the final ballot, Clark won only 38% of the under-30 delegates, while Mulroney won 58%.[25] The elastic nature of electing youth delegates, allowed by the Conservative party constitution, quite literally saved the Mulroney candidacy.

Though he ran as an urban progressive in 1976, Mulroney had positioned himself as a candidate of the right by 1983. As the president of the Iron Ore Company, he could talk about his private-sector experience to a party that fervently believed in private enterprise. Without endorsing explicit right-wing policies, like the flat tax, Mulroney used the rhetoric of the right. This strategy paid off: 52% of Mulroney's supporters wanted to move to the right compared to 18% of Clark's.[26] Clark had the center, Mulroney ended up with the right and, in 1983, the right was considerably larger.

While using the right to dethrone Clark, Mulroney used his fluency in French and appeal in Quebec to blunt the challenge of Crosbie. His formula for a Conservative victory — that the Tories could not give the Liberals 100 francophone seats and expect to win — was a powerful appeal. It distinguished him from the uni-lingual Crosbie and, when the Newfoundlander made the mistake of raising the language issue late in the campaign, it was a godsend to Mulroney.

John Crosbie's 639 votes on the first ballot were an impressive total but not close enough to Mulroney to make him the focus of the anyone-but-Clark coalition. Crosbie had more potential second-ballot support than anyone, but he had to be in a position to overtake Clark. Peter Pocklington told Crosbie that if he were within 200 votes of Mulroney, he would move to the Crosbie camp.

Crosbie wasn't, and Pocklington didn't. One overriding factor caused Crosbie's loss. He was unilingual. And 75% of the Tory delegates believed it was important that the next leader speak French.[27] To win, the Tories had to be more competitive in Quebec. To be competitive in Quebec, they required a bilingual leader. This desire to win served both to bring down Clark and prevent John Crosbie from becoming his challenger.

Each of the three main candidates had a plausible scenario for victory, but each needed a different opponent. Joe Clark needed to face John Crosbie on the final ballot. In 1976, 70% of Mulroney's support had come to Clark, giving him a slender margin over Wagner. In 1983, Clark had split Quebec's 726 votes down the middle with Mulroney. If the Quebecker were no longer in the race and facing a unilingual opponent, Clark could hope for a sweep from Quebec. If he could hold his loyal plateau of 1,050, the 350 Mulroney votes from Quebec would give him a chance. Ian Macdonald, Mulroney's biographer, has written perceptively that Clark's only chance was to divert enough of his loyal votes temporarily to Crosbie on the third ballot to allow the Newfoundlander to pass Mulroney.[28] But Clark's margin was too thin and this maneuver would require discipline that not even Joe Clark's troops could muster.

John Crosbie, on the other hand, needed to face Brian Mulroney. He made desperate appeals to Joe Clark to withdraw on his behalf. With the anyone-but-Mulroney factor almost as large as the anyone-but-Clark coalition, Crosbie might have received between 600 and 650 votes from Clark and, even though Clark's 350 Quebec votes would have gone to Mulroney, the spread would have favored the Newfoundlander. Indeed, a private Mulroney poll forecast that in a Crosbie-Mulroney showdown, the Newfoundlander would win 44.4% to 35.6%.[29]

In order to win, Brian Mulroney needed to face Joe Clark on the last ballot — and so it proved. He knew that at least two-thirds of John Crosbie's delegates would favor him over Clark. Mulroney's strategy was to be close enough to Clark to become the recipient of the anti-Clark coalition votes, but not to pass Clark until the last ballot to keep the anyone-but-Mulroney factor from coming into play. He was 235 votes ahead of Crosbie on the first ballot, enough of a margin that Pocklington and Wilson came to him. While the former supporters of Wilson and Pocklington gave him only 50% of their vote, that was enough to maintain his margin over Crosbie. When Crosbie had to withdraw after the third ballot his support came to Mulroney by a margin of two to one. In the end, it turned out to be anyone but Clark.

CONCLUSION

In 1983, the Conservative party rendered judgment on Joe Clark. He had lost the caucus. He still retained the support of the party establishment, but in a showdown vote in his party, a majority of the 3,000 delegates had turned against their leader by a split of 55% to 45%. Brian Mulroney skillfully exploited the youth loophole of the Conservative constitution to overcome his weakness among English-speaking riding delegates and substantially improved upon his Quebec showing of 1976. Moving with the times, he appeared as a candidate of the right and used that movement's grievances to forge the anti-Clark coalition.

Thus Mulroney adroitly fished in the negative waters of the right. But the heart of his candidacy was a positive appeal to the Conservative party to end the Liberal ascendancy by challenging the Liberals in their heartland of Quebec. That was the promise and the gamble of the Mulroney campaign. The Conservative delegates were asked to dethrone a leader from their traditional base of Western Canada, with all the bitterness that would entail, in the hope of displacing the Liberals in Quebec. It was a gamble that the Conservative party accepted.

4

Picking a Winner

The 3,442 Liberals meeting in Ottawa on June 13-16, 1984, were in an upbeat mood. Their incumbent leader, Pierre Trudeau, had resigned gracefully on February 29, 1984, a civil exit that contrasted starkly with the bloody dethronement of Joe Clark. The delegate-selection process for the convention had proceeded smoothly with none of the embarrassing publicity that had marred the Conservative effort a year before. Two strong candidates, John Napier Turner and Jean Chrétien, had emerged, ensuring that the delegates would be participating in a contest rather than a coronation. Most of all, by the spring, the Liberal party had finally begun to rebound from the depths of their recession-induced unpopularity. In March, a Goldfarb poll showed the party rebounding, capturing 42% of voters. It was the party's best showing since September 1981, and other published polls were confirming the same trend.

Nearly three-quarters of the delegates thought the chances were excellent to good that the party would again form a majority government.[1] The polls, the timing, the atmosphere and the candidates all seemed to demonstrate that the Liberals had not lost their touch. They would continue to be the governing party.

But the sunny optimism of June belied the actual state of the party. The Liberals, in fact, faced a daunting political challenge. In power for all but nine months of the preceding 21 years, the party had to finesse that most basic of political yearnings — the proverbial "time for a change." The desire for a change was natural enough after 21 years, but recent events had considerably sharpened the desire of the populace for a different approach. In the recession of 1981–82, Canada had faced the worst economic crisis since the Depression; as interest rates soared and unemployment increased, the popularity of the Trudeau government plummeted. By January 1982, private Liberal polls showed the Conservatives leading the Liberals by 45% to 29% of the popular vote and, although a return to better times and the Trudeau peace initiative had somewhat restored the lustre of the government (public support for the Liberals climbed to 36% in January 1984 from 29% in January 1982), it was clear that public disenchantment with the government was deep-rooted.

What many people misunderstood was that the desire for change was not a desire for radical change in the policy direction of the government. The negativism toward the Trudeau government was not a result of the government's policies as much as it was of Trudeau's personality and style of governing. For the most part, the policies pursued under Trudeau — such as the National Energy Program, the Foreign Investment Review Agency and various social policies — were supported, as Table I below indicates. People did not want to see much in the way of change insofar as the Liberal party's fundamental policy positions were concerned, particularly the Liberal party's position on social policy. They wanted the government to continue to be in the middle of the political spectrum, and did not want it to move to the right.[2]

But Canadians did want a different approach to leadership and, most of all, they wanted a new approach to managing economic, not social issues. People wanted new fresh faces and ideas to be brought forward. In fact, they wanted more the perception of change in the form of new faces and ideas, than the reality of change in the form of a change in policy direction.

In fulfilling people's expectations for change, the Liberal party needed to be careful to differentiate between what people resented or respected about Trudeau's personality and his government's policies. The dilemma facing the party as it went into the 1984 leadership convention was how to respond to the desire for change without repudiating the past.

The Conservatives, too, had complicated an already difficult Liberal task by electing a Quebecker as leader. The Tories had taken a major gamble in dumping Joe Clark, a westerner who represented their core base of support, in favor of Brian Mulroney, a man who based his challenge on the premise that he could win in Quebec. For the first time since the era of George Etienne-Cartier, the Conservatives had a credible presence in Quebec. Rock solid support in that province — the foundation of Liberal success since

Laurier — could no longer be taken for granted. The Liberals had to respond to a widespread desire for newness while at the same

Support For Liberal Party Policy Positions,
September 1983 – May 1984

	% of Canadians
Economic Policy	
For the federal government spending more money to create jobs as opposed to leaving that responsibility to the private sector	64
Oppose raising taxes to reduce the deficit	73
For focusing more on creating employment than decreasing the federal deficit	67
Social Welfare Policy	
For increasing pensions	87
Oppose cutting back on unemployment insurance to reduce the deficit	62
Oppose cutting back on welfare to reduce the deficit	55
For promoting greater equality for women's salaries	80
For *not* allowing extra billing by doctors and hospitals	80
Foreign Investment/FIRA	
Future foreign investment should be more tightly controlled	58
Support existence of FIRA	56
Energy Policy/NEP/Petro Canada	
Support increasing the level of Canadian ownership of the oil industry in Canada	74
Opposed to allowing Canada's oil to rise to world levels	71
Oppose selling Petro Canada	53
Defense	
For *not* increasing Canada's defense spending	60

Table I

time defending their traditional fortress. To succeed they would need a subtle blend of change and continuity. The two major contenders each offered a different formula.

John Turner represented a repudiation of the Trudeau legacy while harkening back to the more distant St. Laurent-Pearson past. The accent of the Turner campaign was on change: change in policies — a new focus on deficit reduction, revision of the NEP and FIRA; change in approach — Pearsonian consensus rather than Trudeau confrontation; and change in regional emphasis — a new priority on the West instead of Quebec. To respond to the 1980s, the Turner team argued, the party should return to the verities of the 1950s.

The Turner campaign sent out signals that they wanted to attract different or new kinds of Liberals — upscale, business people and Western Canadians. The Turner campaign became so caught up in trying to attract this new Liberal constituency that, to a large extent, it lost sight of or ignored the loyal core constituency and the traditional backbone of the Liberal party: that is, ethnics, middle to lower-income earners, women, baby-boomers, francophones and Ontario Liberals. This would come back to haunt Turner in the ill-fated federal election later that year.

The Turner strategists had misread the mood for change and the type of change that Canadians wanted. Canadians wanted a new leader and new style of leadership, not a radical change in policy direction. They did not want the Liberal party to move to the right.

If Turner's accent was on change, Chrétien's was on continuity. Jean Chrétien promised more of the same, but delivered in a different way. He defended the Trudeau record with pride, emphasized the Trudeau priorities and offered the best hope of maintaining the traditional base of Quebec. Chrétien's "newness" was in his style. Breezy, irreverent, non-intellectual, Chrétien was that rarest of plants in the Liberal soil — a genuine populist. Representing Shawinigan, a mill town in the region of Quebec that had spawned populists such as Maurice Duplessis, Réal Caouette, and Camille Samson, Chrétien may have supported the Trudeau policy, but his personality could not have offered a more vivid contrast to the aloof, intellectual, elite Montrealer. Chrétien's gregarious affection for *les petits gars* and disdain for elaborate planning systems and structure of all kinds made him the first populist since John Diefenbaker with a chance to lead a major party.

While Chrétien made no apologies for the Trudeau era, Turner implied that there was an element of shame for him in the Trudeau record. In the end this hurt Turner, not so much at the convention, but in the ensuing election campaign. His reluctance to accept that the country genuinely liked the fundamental policy direction pursued under Trudeau was instrumental in the Liberal party's defeat.

The Liberal convention of June 1984 certainly lacked the drama of the Conservative gathering a year earlier. No leader was deposed, there were only two ballots, the acknowledged front-runner, John Turner, won an easy victory and there was none of the frantic maneuvering that had characterized the epic Clark-Mulroney-Crosbie confrontation. But behind the surface calm, the Liberal party wrestled with its own soul. Did the delegates want to win above all else, even if it meant choosing a man they thought to be on the extreme right of the party, or did they want to preserve the glories of the recent past with a man whose qualities they loved but whose capabilities they doubted? The answer to that question was delivered decisively on June 16.

WINNING HABITS

The secret of political success, W. L. Mackenzie King once told Lester Pearson, is not what you do right but what you avoid doing wrong. King's formula for never doing wrong rested on brokerage: if one could include all major interests within the party, then conflicts could be managed internally, allowing the party to present a unified front to the public. Through King's long tenure (1919 to 1948) the Liberal party developed a distinct operating style and internal code of behavior. Loyalty to the leader was the norm, reconciliation of French and English Canada was the priority and internal consensus-building was the favored process.[3]

This Liberal code continues as the ideal even today. Two recent books by prominent Liberals demonstrate the thesis. Roy MacLaren, minister of state for finance in the Trudeau government, writes in *Consensus* that the Liberal party is a kind of school: "It has a multiplicity of interests. It is a good training ground for the art of governing, which is itself a process of harmonizing contending interests in such a way as to win the broad consent of the government."[4]

John Roberts, a veteran Liberal cabinet minister of the Trudeau era, subtitles one of the chapters in his *Agenda for Canada,* "The Need for Brokerage Politics." Brokerage, Roberts writes, "corresponds to the geographic, social, and economic diversity of our country and to the need for consensus and reconciliation, and it is especially important in view of the planning function which government must perform."[5]

This steady devotion to the values of consensus, reconciliation and accommodation produced a Liberal party culture strikingly at variance with that of the Conservative party. It was the government-party-versus-the-Tory syndrome. Data from the 1983 and 1984 conventions make the point. The recent history of the Conservative party has been marked by a radical right-wing surge in the policy preferences of party militants, bitter disputes among factions, resulting in significant portions of the party (25%) favoring anybody but Clark or anybody but Mulroney, and hotly contested delegation meetings where fist fights broke out and extraordinary packing of the convention with youth delegates occurred.

None of the above characterized the Liberal convention of 1984. Delegates were chosen without incident, the loopholes in the party constitution were not abused in any undue way, the senior Liberal contenders were well regarded even by their rivals and the policy instincts of Liberal activists from 1968 to 1984 demonstrated continuity. Like the Conservatives, Liberal partisans put a premium on winning, but unlike the Tories they developed an operating style that complemented that objective instead of thwarting it.

Of the 3,442 accredited delegates to the 1984 convention, 51% were elected from the ridings, 27% were ex officio and 22% were youth delegates (1,740, 940 and 762 delegates respectively). If youth delegates were the critical dimension of the Tory convention (the Tories had 200 more youth delegates — 972 to 762 — than their Liberal counterparts) the major story of the Liberal convention was that the party had finally given women a fair break. In 1984, 1,382 female delegates were accredited, compared to 10 in the Liberal leadership convention of 1919 and 27 in the leadership convention of 1948. Women made up 50% of the elected riding delegates, but there was a significant disparity among the youth delegation and a huge imbalance among the ex-officio representatives.[6]

The importance of women in the Liberal party was reflected in the stands that all candidates took on issues such as equal pay for work of equal value. The policy proposition that ranked first in delegate support advocated greater equality for women's salaries: 90% of the delegates favored this measure with only 8% opposed.[7]

The serenity of the delegate election process was matched by the benign view held by most delegates of the major contenders. Liberal delegates had a high opinion of their main leadership choices. Both Chrétien and Turner ranked higher in Liberal hearts than Clark and Mulroney did among the Tory faithful.[8]

Average Impression Ranking

	Maximum = 10		
Jean Chrétien	7.7	Joe Clark	6.4
John Turner	7.5	Brian Mulroney	6.2

Table II

The partisans of Chrétien and Turner also thought relatively highly of their opponents, relative to the bitterness of the Tory fight. Turner delegates rated Chrétien at 7 and Chrétien delegates put Turner at 6.1. Mulroney delegates, however, rated Joe Clark at only 4.4, while Clark's followers deemed Mulroney worth only a 4.3.

The general satisfaction of Liberals with their candidates is also reflected in the size of the faction who stated that they would never vote for the leading contenders under any circumstances: 26% of the Tories rejected Clark and 25% Mulroney in those terms. Only 12% of Liberals were similarly negative about John Turner and just 11% felt the same about Jean Chrétien. Most Liberals were generally content with their top two leadership candidates.[9]

Average Impression Ranking Among Delegates' First Choice

	Total	Chrétien	Turner	All Others
		(Maximum	= 10)	
Chrétien	7.7	8.9	7.0	7.2
Turner	7.5	6.1	8.8	6.6
	Total	Clark	Mulroney	All Others
Clark	6.4	9.3	4.4	5.6
Mulroney	6.2	4.3	9.1	6.4

Table III

The positive attitude demonstrated by the Liberal delegates toward these two candidates was to have negative — and serious — repercussions on the destiny of the Liberal party in the near future. During Turner's electoral campaign and after his defeat in 1984, his supporters failed both to understand and to take into account the considerable grassroots support that Chrétien had generated. The 1984 convention drama was not about a struggle between two personalities; it was the tale of a struggle between representatives of two different visions of Canada, of two different value systems, of two divergent stands on many issues. In the denouement of the 1984 Liberal convention, Turner's main difficulty was to be the almost insurmountable challenge of refocussing his own value system and realigning it with traditional Liberal beliefs.

POLICY STABILITY

If the story of the Conservative party in recent years tells of a dramatic shift towards the right in the values of party activists, the Liberal party story demonstrated instead an almost complete policy continuity. In 1968, a survey of delegates to the convention that chose Pierre Trudeau revealed three main findings:

*the Liberal party was strongly centralist and favored federal government activism;

*there was wide support for the welfare state and an eagerness to extend it;
*party members were evenly divided on whether the government should intervene in the economy and were especially split on the subject of foreign investment.

In 1984, the Liberal party had exactly the same profile as it did in 1968: the party favored social security and strong federal leadership in federal/provincial relations, but was split down the middle on how best to respond to American economic dominance.[10]

Articles on the 1968 Liberal leadership are many but assessments of the delegates attending that convention are few. Professors J. Lele, G. C. Perlin and H. G. Thorburn of Queen's University, undertook one such study and Table IV compares the 1968 and 1984 results.[11]

Specific issues change, but the overall policy orientation of the Liberal party changed little from the 1960s to the 1980s. As the party of national unity, the Liberals promoted bilingualism in the 1960s and in 1984 by a margin of two to one and they supported the federal government's ensuring minority language rights rather than allowing the provinces primacy in this regard. In 1968, 77% of delegates favored a strong central government and in 1984, by a margin of 75% to 14%, the delegates wanted the federal government to "take charge where federal-provincial confrontation occurs."

By supporting medicare in 1968 and disagreeing with the view that government spent too much on social welfare, this social-security dimension of Liberal policy had strengthened even further by 1984. Delegates favored a guaranteed annual income by a margin of two to one, by 74% to 20% they wanted to raise old-age pensions, and by a margin of three to one, they rejected the idea that the federal deficit should be reduced by cutting back on welfare, unemployment insurance or foreign aid. The social conscience of the Liberal party continued to be as strong as its centralism.

Policy Preferences, Liberal Delegates 1968 and 1984

		% of Liberal delegates	
		1968	1984
Federal-Provincial Powers			
Provincial government should have more power	Agree	15	12
	Disagree	77	78
For a stronger central government to take charge in federal-provincial confrontations	Agree	N/A	75
	Disagree	N/A	14
Social Welfare			
Old age pensions and baby bonus should only be given to people who need them	Agree	51	35
	Disagree	43	62
For a guaranteed income for needy Canadians	Agree	N/A	66
	Disagree	N/A	28
Government has a responsibility to help people not able to look after themselves	Agree	94	N/A
	Disagree	3	N/A
Free medicare available to everyone	Agree	50	N/A
	Disagree	43	N/A
For prohibiting extra billing by doctors in medicare system	Agree	N/A	83
	Disagree	N/A	13
For reducing the federal deficit by cutting back on unemployment insurance benefits	Agree	N/A	24
	Disagree	N/A	71
For reducing the federal deficit by cutting back on welfare	Agree	N/A	22
	Disagree	N/A	72
For increasing pensions	Agree	N/A	74
	Disagree	N/A	20

Policy Preferences, Liberal Delegates 1968 and 1984

		% of Liberal delegates	
		1968	1984
Language Rights			
French-speaking Canadians outside Quebec should be able to use French when they deal with their own government	Agree Disagree	73 21	N/A N/A
For federal government intervention over provincial objections in the assurance of language rights	Agree Disagree	N/A N/A	63 29
Economic Issues			
We ought to seek greater American investment in Canada	Agree Disagree	55 33	N/A N/A
For special laws to regulate foreign investment	Agree Disagree	66 28	N/A N/A
For increased open trade with the United States	Agree Disagree	N/A N/A	46 47
Government ought to interfere less with business	Agree Disagree	35 51	N/A N/A
Reduce corporate taxes with an attendant cut in government services	Agree Disagree	N/A N/A	23 69
Make Canadair survive on its own	Agree Disagee	N/A N/A	46 42
For the federal government spending more money to create jobs as opposed to leaving that responsibility to the private sector	Agree Disagree	N/A N/A	51 40

Foreign Aid

Devote more money to aid	Agree	63	61
the underdeveloped countries	Disagree	27	34

Defense

Spend less on defense	Agree	67	N/A
	Disagree	24	N/A
Increase Canadian	Agree	N/A	43
defense spending	Disagree	N/A	52

Table IV

In 1966, the followers of Walter Gordon and Mitchell Sharp had battled in the Liberal policy convention over medicare and foreign investment. The results were inconclusive: the Gordon wing succeeded in persuading the convention that medicare could be delayed at most for one year and the Sharp forces plainly had convinced a majority at the convention to reject a strong motion advocating restrictions on foreign investment. The Gordon wing withdrew its resolution and a compromise resolution was passed instead.

This early fight over foreign investment symbolized an important division within the Liberal ranks. Liberal activists are largely united on French-English language issues, the Constitution and social policy, but with respect to the role of the state in regulating the economy, there are sharp differences. William Christian and Colin Campbell have identified property, or business liberalism, versus social democratic, or welfare liberalism, as one of the critical cleavages in the party,[12] and the 1984 data confirms that this policy debate continues. Of the 10 issues that most divided the party, six related to this business-versus-welfare dimension. Free trade, support for Crown corporations, the role of the private sector in creating jobs and the importance of the deficit were the most hotly contested issues. On the deficit, for example, 51% deemed reducing it to be a priority, while 46% did not; 46% wanted free general trade with the United States, while 47% were content with the existing trade policy.[13]

Policy Preferences, Liberal Delegates, 1984 Convention

	% of Liberal Delegates	
	Agree	Disagree
Economic Issues		
For increased open trade with the U.S.	46	47
For the federal government stepping in to save deHavilland	44	39
For the federal government spending more money to create jobs as opposed to leaving that responsibility to the private sector	51	40
For the federal government stepping in to save Canadair	42	46
Perceive decreasing the deficit as a critical issue	51	46

Table V

During the 1968 convention, Robert Winters, Paul Hellyer and Mitchell Sharp were firmly identified with the business wing. John Turner, Paul Martin and Joe Green were in the center. Pierre Trudeau, Allan MacEachen and Eric Kierans were identified as being on the left. Trudeau won decisively in a fourth-ballot showdown with Winters. In 1984, the Liberal party was even more decidedly liberal in its social policy outlook and in its eagerness to use the federal government to protect minority rights. But these policy values ran headlong into an equally strong desire to succeed electorally. In 1968, Trudeau was perceived to be both a reformer and a winner. In 1984, the perceived winner, John Turner, was now firmly identified as a man of the right — even of the extreme right — of the party he sought to lead. He, in fact, was considered the most right-leaning candidate of all the leadership contenders, rated by delegates at 6.2 on the right-left scale where a rating of 10 represented the far right and a rating of 1, the far left.[14]

Something would have to give — the policy consensus around social welfare and language rights, or the party's passion to retain power. In the end, the passion for power won out.

THE RESTORATION OF JOHN TURNER

When John Turner announced on March 16, 1984 that he would contest the Liberal leadership, he had been absent from active politics since 1976. Despite this stretch of time — Harold Wilson once said that a week is an eternity in politics — Turner was the acknowledged front-runner. More than that, the media,[15] the power brokers within the party and conventional wisdom thought him so far in front that the question was not whether he would win, but whether there would even be a contest. The Toronto lawyer's ability to remain the crown prince of the Liberal party throughout the Trudeau era was a testament to the tremendous reputation Turner had gained as a minister from 1967 through 1975. As Canada's economic woes deepened and the party's political fortunes worsened, Turner seemed to many to be the one ace in the hole in the Liberal party.

Turner first ran for the leadership of the Liberal party in 1968. In that contest, at the age of 38, he ran as a representative of a new age, promising reform and demonstrating personal dynamism. The John Turner of 1968 would have horrified his business supporters of 1984. After entering the cabinet on April 4, 1967 (along with two other newcomers — Pierre Trudeau and Jean Chrétien) Turner gave an interview to Pierre Berton in which he supported a guaranteed annual income, a capital-gains tax, and the abolition of university tuition fees.[16] Turner entered the 1968 leadership campaign hoping to be the candidate of the Liberal reformers, but this terrain was soon occupied by Pierre Trudeau. Turner, however, ran a credible campaign, finishing third to Trudeau and Winters, and was generally regarded as a man to watch.

His performance in the portfolios of justice and finance added to his reputation. While in justice, he was careful to make non-partisan appointments to the bench, he created the Law Reform Commission and he steered the Official Languages Act through the House. Appointed to the finance portfolio in 1972, he skillfully brought down budgets that combined popular tax breaks such as the Registered Home Ownership Savings Plan (RHOSP) with supply-side measures such as cuts in corporate revenue tax and indexation of the tax system. Turner's desire to return to private life led to his resignation in 1975. His resignation rocked the Trudeau government and weakened its standing in financial circles in English Canada.

From 1976 to 1984, Turner practised law in Toronto, joined several corporate boards, emerged occasionally to make speeches critical of the Trudeau government's economic or constitutional policies and saw his reputation gain strength with every passing year.

Turner's standing in the party was grounded in the strength of his image in the country. After 16 years of Pierre Trudeau, Canadians wanted their next leader to be different. As the old adage goes, democracies tend to choose a leader who is the exact opposite of his or her predecessor. Thus, Nixon "the crook" was replaced by Carter "the moralist" and Carter "the wimp" was replaced by Reagan "the cowboy". After Trudeau, the French-Canadian intellectual who made national unity his priority and confrontation his style, many Canadians longed for an English-Canadian man of business who would make the economy the priority and consensus the goal. This description fit both John Turner and Brian Mulroney like a glove.

ALTERNATING LEADERS

A phrase repeatedly heard throughout the Liberal leadership campaign was "It's English Canada's turn." Liberals deny that there should be an inflexible rule that French and English leaders should alternate, but since Laurier the tradition has held fast. Both in 1968 and in 1984, less than a third of the delegates thought alternating was a good idea, but even if only a quarter to a third of the convention was influenced by this factor, it was a significant advantage.[17] In 1984, 27% thought the party should continue to alternate between French and English leaders and 70% were opposed, but a significant number of Turner supporters — not surprisingly — supported the idea; 40% of the delegates favoring Turner on the first ballot favored alternating, compared to only 10% of those wanting Chrétien. Most delegates (70%) believed that the best individual, regardless of ethnicity, should be chosen, but the alternation tradition did assist both Trudeau in 1968 and Turner in 1984. Chrétien's chances were not helped by Marc Lalonde's comment that deviating from the alternating tradition could jeopardize the future opportunity for Quebec candidates to attain the leadership of the party.

LEANING RIGHT

Business Liberals, who favor the party's position on national unity but are less inclined to support social security and who are actually opposed to state intervention in the economy, traditionally make up between a quarter and a third of party activists. In 1968, 35% of the delegates thought the government should intervene less with business, 27% voted to cut foreign aid and 28% disagreed that there should be special laws to regulate foreign investment.[18] In 1984, a similar pattern emerged: 28% of the delegates opposed a guaranteed income, 32% wanted to raise taxes to reduce the federal deficit and 35% favored the application of a means test for social programs. This third of the party voted overwhelmingly for Robert Winters in 1968, and they provided a natural base for the Turner candidacy in 1984.

The strategy of the Turner forces was to emphasize change and renewal, and to put distance between the Trudeau record and Turner. They would attract most of that third of the party who had opposed Pierre Trudeau at the beginning and who had always been uneasy with the interventionist or nationalistic initiatives of the Trudeau government. With that base secure, Turner would gain a majority by attracting moderate Liberals who wanted to win above all else, and who saw him as the best candidate to achieve that end.

At his press conference announcing his candidacy for the leadership, Turner's strategy was evident. He attacked the advisors of Trudeau and promised a different style of leadership and a more open party. He responded to a question about language rights by emphasizing the role of the provinces — a clear departure from the stance of the Trudeau government. And, most importantly for his constituency, he promised to cut the deficit in half within seven years. Making an attack upon the deficit his first priority served to put distance between Turner and the Trudeau government. Turner later softened his original hard-line position. By the end of the leadership campaign, deficit reduction was rarely mentioned by the front-runner. His initial position, however, had already served its purpose: by emphasizing deficit reduction early on, Turner had sewn up the business Liberals and could now concentrate on wooing the moderates.

Reflecting Liberal homogeneity on most issues, the supporters of Chrétien and Turner exhibited few differences. But where differences did exist, they usually reflected the stronger business Liberal element in the Turner camp. On a host of issues, by a margin of five to seven percentage points, the Turner camp was more conservative than the Chrétien camp. Thus, 31% of Turner delegates rejected a guaranteed annual income, compared to 24% of Chrétien supporters; 27% of Turner's delegates wanted to cut unemployment insurance to reduce the deficit, compared to 22% of Chrétien's people; while 37% of Turner's delegates favored a means test for social services, compared to 32% of Chrétien's. A majority of delegates in both the Turner and Chrétien camps favored the social-welfare positions as opposed to the minority business Liberal school, but individuals adhering to this school of conservative persuasion clustered together in Turner's corner. They provided the core strength of his candidacy.

The two issues that polarized the two camps were the deficit and minority language rights. Table VI summarizes these positions. In each case, the pattern was the same: Turner delegates were at one end of the spectrum and Chrétien delegates at another, with the supporters of the five other candidates falling in the middle, (although leaning toward the Chrétien position).[19]

Brokerage politics in the King model suggests not only that all interests should be represented, but also that parties should move according to the prevailing political winds. King's own actions in committing the Liberal party firmly to the welfare state, after a 1943 Gallup poll showed that a plurality of the country supported the CCF, is a case in point. True to this political heritage in the era of Thatcher and Reagan, Liberal delegates favored shifting the party slightly to the right, even though they individually supported liberal positions on almost every issue surveyed. Turner's clear identification with the right, therefore, was not a disadvantage in the eyes of delegates because that is where they thought the party should go. The question was one of degree — was Turner too far right?

Policy Views Of Turner And Chrétien Delegates

	All Liberal Delegates	Turner Delegates	Chrétien Delegates	Other Candidates Delegates
1. For decreasing federal deficit	51	58	41	43
Not a critical issue in your mind	46	38	56	51
2. For federal government intervention over provincial objections in the assurance of minority language rights	63	56	74	66
For minority language rights as a provincial matter	29	38	19	27

Table VI

Table VII summarizes the preference of Liberal delegates and, most interestingly, shows that Quebec Liberals were more conservative than Liberals in the rest of the country.[20] In 1984, Quebeckers wished to move the party significantly right. This undoubtedly reflected provincial politics in Quebec, where the Liberal party of Quebec faced the Parti Québécois, a party aspiring to a social-democratic label. Quebec delegates also had a more benign view of the Conservatives compared to Western Liberals who, having experienced the real thing, placed the Conservative party to the extreme right of the spectrum. Turner delegates were the most conservative and favored the greatest shift in Liberal party stance.

Scaling Of The Liberal Party

	Liberal Party Is	Self-Identification	Conservative Party Is	Liberal Party Should Be
Total	5.2	5.4	6.7	5.5
Region				
West	4.9	5.3	7.6	5.3
Ontario	5.0	5.2	7.2	5.2
Quebec	6.0	5.8	5.4	6.2
Atlantic	5.0	5.3	6.5	5.3
Language				
English	5.0	5.2	7.1	5.3
French	6.0	5.8	5.4	6.2
Sex				
Male	5.0	5.3	6.9	5.4
Female	5.5	5.4	6.5	5.7
Age				
Under 25	5.1	5.2	6.4	5.4
25-44	5.2	5.2	7.0	5.4
45 +	5.3	5.6	6.6	5.7
Candidate Supported				
Turner	5.3	5.6	6.7	5.7
Chrétien	5.3	5.3	6.4	5.5
All others	4.8	5.0	7.2	5.1

Table VII

Liberal delegates viewed John Turner at 6.2 in the left-right scale, not far from where they placed the Conservative party at 6.7. This was considerably further than their self-identification positioning of 5.4 and of their indication of where they thought the Liberal party should position itself, at 5.5. Even Turner delegates who positioned themselves at 5.6 believed their champion was more to the right than they were by placing him at 6.1. Tactically, Liberals thought they should swing from the center to the center-right, but they worried that Turner would take them too far in that direction. The Chrétien camp needed to play on these doubts. The Turner forces had to overcome them by focussing on John Turner, the winner.

WANTING A WINNER

In 1984 the Liberal party had formed the government of Canada for all but nine months of the preceding 21 years. Its devotion to winning required little emphasis. Like the Conservative delegates a year before, Liberal delegates placed a heavy, but not predominant, emphasis on the candidate's ability to win. Out of an average of 10 points, the Liberal delegates placed 4.3 points on the candidate's stand on issues, 3.3 points on his ability to beat the Conservatives and 2.4 points on personality. Turner delegates placed the highest premium on winning, placing it at 3.7 points, compared to 3.1 points for Chrétien delegates.

Pierre Trudeau had announced that 1980 would be his last campaign and, from that date, polls had periodically tested the political futures of the two major parties with John Turner as the hypothetical leader of the Liberal party. The impact of Turner's past performance as a minister and his continuing hold on the press and public was dramatically evidenced by these pre-leadership polls. In January 1983, for example, at a time when the Liberal party was running nearly 20 points behind the Conservatives (49 to 31), a Gallup survey showed that the Liberals under John Turner would defeat the Conservatives under Joe Clark. The perceived ability of John Turner to add 10 to 15 points to the Liberal total was a key consideration in the decision of the Conservatives to replace Joe Clark with Brian Mulroney.

The public's strong perception of Turner's leadership abilities made him an obvious object of media attention. This, in turn, added to his image as a winner. Both the media and the polls broadcast the same message — if the Liberal party wanted to win again and put behind it the recession of 1981 and 1982, the easiest way to do it was to choose John Turner.

Turner's preeminent position in the media and in the public eye not only helped him with the delegates, but also scared off other potential strong candidates. Who did *not* run in the Liberal leadership race was as important to the final outcome as those who eventually did. Fully 30% of the delegates in 1984 indicated that they would have supported another candidate who was not in the fold. Iona Campagnola had two-thirds of this potentially large base.[21] Lloyd Axworthy was another Western non-candidate with potential support from delegates. Had Campagnola and Axworthy run, they would have cut into Turner's Western base and ensured a multi-balloted convention. But Axworthy eventually became Turner's campaign manager and supplied early help when Turner had difficulty in putting together his own team. While in 1968 four of five strong candidates tried for the leadership, in 1984 there were really two, and support for the five other contenders was so thin that there was little room for convention maneuvering.

Turner's potential as a Liberal winner also helped in a most direct way with a critical group of delegates. Nearly 1,000 Liberal delegates were ex-officio members appointed or elected to party executives under the leadership of Pierre Trudeau. In the 1983 Conservative contest, the ex officios strongly supported Joe Clark, unsurprisingly since he had appointed them. In 1984 John Turner had deliberately disassociated himself from the Trudeau record, but, by a margin of three to one, these ex officios supported the man who spent much of his time criticizing the leader who had given them their place.[22]

Why? These ex-officio leaders were the Liberal party's power brokers and professionals. They placed the highest premium on winning. In part, their positions in the government, their boards and their directorships depended upon it. They went en masse with the supposed winner. Jean Chrétien gave Turner a competitive fight in the constituency contests for delegates, but the ex officios gave Turner his most substantial lead. The party establishment voted for its greatest critic because they thought he was the one man who could deliver what they desired most — power. Survey results in Professor George Perlin's *Party Democracy in Canada* reveal that on the showdown second ballot, 61.7% of the ex officios voted for Turner, compared with 26.6% for Chrétien. Constituency, youth and women delegates, in contrast, showed a closer margin — 54.8% for Turner and 35.1% for Chrétien.[23]

THE POPULIST CHALLENGE

On March 16, 1984, when John Turner announced his candidacy, it appeared that the Liberal convention would be a coronation. By the opening of the convention on June 14, though, it had become a contest. This was due both to a series of Turner gaffes, brilliantly exploited by his main opponent, and the intrinsic merits of Jean Chrétien's high-spirited populist background.

Chrétien had had some important demerits going into the campaign. He was a francophone trying to overcome the party's alternation tradition. He was intimately associated with the Trudeau government, when both party and public thought it was time for a change. He was a populist backwoodsman from Shawinigan, not held in high repute in the intellectual circles of Montreal.

This became Chrétien's Achilles' heel; he could command significant caucus support from neither the anglophones nor the francophones. And without caucus support, Chrétien would not be able to muster the ex-officio support a candidate required. Because Chrétien could not get the caucus support he needed, his stature was never legitimized, either to the delegates, or to the population at large.

But Chrétien had some assets, too. He had traveled back and forth across the country in the seven years that John Turner had been away, and many in the party owed him debts for campaign and fund-raising favors. He was a natural orator, able to stir a crowd. And, most of all, there was his own personality — funny, cheerful and street-smart. People liked Jean Chrétien.

Chrétien had devised a strategy that sought to conform to 1984's political realities without repudiating the tradition of the Liberal party. Like John Turner, he had recognized that the party and the country demanded change, but unlike his opponent, he offered a change in style and not in party direction.

Chrétien had made a virtue of necessity and had identified himself with the Trudeau policy legacy. He emphasized jobs, not the deficit, social security rather than business confidence, minority rights rather than provincial rights. His free-wheeling, sunny personality contrasted both with the austere, intellectual Trudeau and the committed, intense and driven Turner. As the party establishment flooded to John Turner's camp, Chrétien made a virtue of this too, and his campaign served as an outlet to all those who worked to *replace* the local party notables. Turner carried the image of a winner, but Chrétien ensured the certainty of carrying Quebec, the fortress of the Liberal party, despite the severity of the Mulroney threat.

Chrétien's strategy was aided by Turner's mistakes. In his first press conference, Turner stumbled over the issue of minority language rights by emphasizing provincial responsibilities rather than active federalism. This was a calculated signal to Western Canadians, but Chrétien used it to good effect in Quebec by suggesting that Turner was abandoning the party's traditional defense of minorities. Turner's rustiness after being out of public life for so long was evident as Chrétien outperformed him at five regional all-candidate meetings organized by the party. Turner entered into a dispute with Pierre Trudeau about his resignation from the cabinet in 1975, and this further upset the Liberal faithful. By the time of the convention, John Turner was no longer regarded as a miracle man; he was mortal after all.

Chrétien made his personality and the policy values of most Liberal delegates work for him. With 60 to 70% of the party opposed to extra billing, opposed to the ending of universality, and opposed to acquiescence to the provinces on minority rights, Chrétien succeeded in identifying himself with those popular positions. Turner was strongly identified with increasing provincial power and moving the Liberal party massively to the right, not the most popular issue positions within the Liberal universe.[24]

Chrétien, too, capitalized on his warm personality: he bested Turner on a number of head-to-head comparisons. Chrétien was viewed as the most believable, trustworthy candidate and the one possessed with the most distinctive personal style. As Table IX demonstrates, however, Turner had two major strengths: Liberals believed he was a winner, that he would win the convention and beat Mulroney, and, like the public, Liberals believed that John Turner had more leadership capability in such crucial spheres as the ability to represent Canada abroad. Chrétien's populism and humor brought him friends, but it left a residue of concern over whether he was serious and weighty enough to be prime minister. This was an underlying Turner strength.[25]

Candidate Most Identified with Policy Position

	Chrétien	Turner
1. For federal government intervention in the assurance of minority language rights	60	14
2. Strong federal government	44	33
3. Promoting bilingualism	66	12
4. More provincial power	9	33
5. Opposes extra billing	31	16
6. Universality for social programs	36	19
7. Increasing Canada's role in NATO	12	31
8. Encouraging the private sector to create jobs	13	52
9. Redirect education spending	14	28
10. Shifting the Liberal party to the right	8	47

Table VIII

Leadership Comparisons

	Chrétien	Turner
1. Sounds most like Mulroney	5	41
2. Most distinctive in terms of style	55	28
3. Most believable on issues	32	33
4. Most opportunistic	12	38
5. Personality you like best	42	30
6. Most comfortable with	41	25
7. Most in tune with your stand on issues	34	38
8. Biggest threat to Mulroney	26	64
9. Will win the convention	26	58
10. Best represents Canada at international economic summits	29	52

Table IX

Chrétien's spirited campaign and Turner's stumbles eventually made an impact on public opinion, but too late to help the Chrétien candidacy. On June 15, the day before the voting, a private poll commissioned by Campeau Associates was released to the Chrétien forces, who promptly gave it to the press. It revealed a dramatic slip in the fortunes of the Liberal party as a result of Turner's performance as a candidate. The poll taken by Goldfarb Consultants in early June showed that unlike every poll taken before Turner announced his candidacy in March (which showed that Turner-led Liberals would defeat the Conservatives) the tables were now turned. The Conservatives were ahead: Liberals 42%, Conservatives 45% and NDP 13%. Under Jean Chrétien, the Liberal party would fare slightly better: Liberals 45%, Conservatives 43%, NDP 12%. Between March and June, the winner had turned into a loser. But the results came too late for Jean Chrétien. John Turner as the easy victor over the Tories was an image too deeply held to be dispelled by one survey. Few — certainly not those in the Turner camp — believed the results. Had they done so, the rush to call an early election after the June convention might have been slowed down.

Turner's performance in the leadership campaign and the new right-of-center policy direction he was advocating for the Liberal party with his emphasis on deficit reduction made Canadians nervous. This was not the kind of change they wanted. The public never really fell in love with John Turner. The delegates at the 1984 leadership convention had misinterpreted the support that the public was prepared to give to Turner. They were never prepared to elect Turner as prime minister in a wholehearted way: he was perceived by the delegates as being much more attractive to the public than he really was. The Liberal party delegates elected Turner on winnability, but the convention had not caught up with the change that had already started to take place in the general public's attitude toward Turner. By the time the Liberal delegates had elected Turner, as the Campeau poll indicated, he had already begun to lose favor with the public.

CHOOSING

John Turner won the June 16 convention easily on the second

ballot. With 1,593 votes on the first ballot, he was only 125 votes short of a majority of 1,718. Chrétien's total of 1,067 was 183 votes short of the 1,250 he needed to make subsequent ballots meaningful. Indeed, even if Chrétien had succeeded in coming close to Turner on a second ballot and had thereby forced a third, the 192 votes of third-place finisher Don Johnston would have decided the outcome. Johnston had voiced many of the same policy themes as Turner and was closer ideologically to the front-runner than to the challenger.

As it turned out, Turner had important supporters in each of the other camps when it came to the second ballot. Although John Munro, Eugene Whelan and John Roberts endorsed Chrétien, many of their followers voted for Turner. On the second ballot, the two leading candidates split additional votes about evenly, with Chrétien gaining 301 and Turner 269 votes.[26]

Turner's victory was a broad one, with substantial support from every region and age category. Chrétien led him decisively in support from the Atlantic and narrowly among people under 25, but Turner won handily everywhere else. Quebec in particular had rejected Chrétien, its native son: Turner led 58% to 40% among French-speaking delegates and 56% to 41% in Quebec as a whole.[27]

The Turner strategy had worked. Starting with a core of perhaps 25% drawn from right-wing business Liberals, Turner had broadened his appeal to win a majority of Quebec delegates. He had softened his image enough so as not to repel moderates who wanted to join the winning team. Had Liberal delegates voted their policy preferences, Chrétien would have won. But they had doubts about Chrétien's leadership abilities and, above all, they saw John Turner as a man who could win.[28]

Party president Iona Campagnola described the contest well when she told the convention moments after Turner's victory that Chrétien had finished second in the votes, "but first in our hearts." Coolly and efficiently, the Liberal party had voted with its head, not its heart, and had made a contract with a winner.

Traditional Liberal values and beliefs were lost in the delegates' overriding concern to retain the spoils of power. What the Liberal party had stood for during the Trudeau years became secondary to the objective of winning and picking a winner.

What the Liberal party was about to learn in the ensuing election was that in politics, the motivation or desire to win is not enough. There has to be a reason to want to be in power. The Liberals lost sight of their reason for wanting power at the 1984 convention and, as a result, suffered the wrath of the public in the subsequent election.

Categories of First-Choice Support of Chrétien and Turner

	Chrétien	Turner
TOTAL	36	49
REGION		
West	32	49
Ontario	30	49
Quebec	41	56
Atlantic	49	39
LANGUAGE		
English	35	58
French	40	51
AGE		
under 25	44	42
25-44	35	47
45 +	33	55

Table X

Reason for Voting	Turner	Chrétien
Because of his stand on issues	31	61
Because of his potential to win	52	24
Would not vote for him under any circumstances	12	11

Table XI

5

A Liberal is a Liberal and a Conservative is a Conservative

The 3,006 accredited delegates to the 1983 Conservative convention and the 3,442 accredited Liberals in 1984 were the shock troops of the Canadian party system. They were the party activists forming one side of the party triangle. The other arms of the triangle were the party leadership and the party voters. These party activists were the men and women who created the policy framework for the parliamentary caucus and formed the extended network of the voluntary party associations. In so doing, they exerted a subtle form of influence on the party leadership. The views of party activists matter.

What is particularly important for Canadian politics is that the views of the activists in our two major parties have grown steadily more distinct with each passing year. Both parties may practise brokerage politics, reaching out to all interests and tacking with the winds of current public opinion, but their core values have become divergent. These differences were apparent from 1967 to 1968 when the two senior parties last held leadership conventions in tandem, but by 1983–84, the rifts were strikingly evident. Since the mid-1960s, the Liberal party has become more liberal in social policy while holding fast to its traditional emphasis on a strong federal government. The Liberals have become slightly more liberal and the Conservatives have become radically more conservative.

The two senior parties still play the game by the same rules, but they are playing for very different goals.

In previous chapters, the method of delegate selection used in the 1983–84 Conservative and Liberal leadership conventions was described and the different credentials of the delegates were compared: 51% of the Liberals were selected by ridings compared to 37% for the Conservatives; 32% of Conservative delegates were young people compared to 22% for the Liberals; and the Conservatives had more automatic or ex officios — 31% to the Liberals' 27%. The regional breakdown, however, was more uniform. Ontario delegates had a slightly larger representation in the Liberal convention, and Newfoundland, showing the impressive results of John Crosbie's youth organizations' efforts, had double the impact in the Tory convention of their provincial counterparts in the Liberal meeting.[1]

THE CONSERVATIVES: PARTY OF THE RIGHT

The Conservative party, as measured by the views of party delegates attending the 1983 leadership convention, is very much a party of the right. In the survey undertaken during the 1983 Conservative convention, issues of greatest consensus for delegates were:

* greater scrutiny of those receiving UIC benefits;
* more open trade with the U.S.;
* testing of the cruise missile;
* parliamentary reform;
* more scrutiny of Crown corporations.

Relative to Liberal delegates, Conservatives place greater trust in business and the free-market system than they do in government to direct the economy and distribute wealth in society. They want government to play a decreased role in the economy and in distributing wealth. They are less committed to maintenance of the social safety net. They place more onus on individuals to take responsibility for their own personal welfare. They reject economic nationalism as an undesirable form of government intervention in the free-market economy. They advocate decentralization of power away from the federal government to the provinces. They are strong proponents of tough law-and-order measures. They advocate a strong military role and presence for Canada, and they are less committed to minority rights.

Conservatives also view the role of government very differently than do Liberals. Liberals believe in active, involved government.

They believe in strong federalism, by which the central government instigates and participates. For Conservatives, however, the federal government acts more as manager than activator, coordinator more than initiator and adjudicator more than participant. (The implications of these interpretations of active versus passive federal powers were to have important implications at the Meech Lake meetings four years later.)

The Conservative party may be a party distinguished by a history of factionalism and personal rivalries, but it is also a party of wide policy consensus. Of the 35 issues on which delegates were surveyed, only five produced significant dissension. As Table I indicates, on most issues there were consensus majorities by a magnitude of two or three to one. Distrust of government and antipathy toward the welfare state are now, and were then, a Conservative article of faith: 87% of the delegates surveyed wanted greater scrutiny of those Canadians receiving unemployment insurance, 73% wanted to tighten control of crown corporations, 68% favored a means test for social programs and 41% wanted to sell Petro-Canada.

The right-leaning orientation of the Conservative party as measured by the attitudes of party delegates is further reflected in the following survey data: 71% favored leaving the responsibility for job creation with the private sector as opposed to government, 64% favored reducing the deficit by cutting back on foreign aid, 67% favored imposing tighter restrictions on immigration, 81% wanted capital punishment reinstated for certain crimes, 55% supported lower taxes with a cut in government services, 72% opposed increasing spending on bilingualism, 72% supported increasing Canada's defense spending, 42% favored reducing the federal deficit by cutting back on welfare and 40% favored reducing the federal deficit by cutting back on unemployment insurance benefits. While standing toe to toe with the Americans in confronting the Soviet Union, and advocating a strong military presence for Canada, Conservative delegates also wanted better economic relations with the U.S.: 77% favored more open trade with the U.S. and 67% wanted to decrease the role of the Foreign Investment Review Agency (FIRA).

Yet while the Conservative party of Brian Mulroney disliked government and certainly no longer favored the extension of the social safety net and welfare state as Robert Stanfield had once advocated, at the same time it held little real enthusiasm for a massive assault on social measures. While the Conservative delegates were clearly much further to the right than the Liberal delegates on social issues, the hard right — those favoring large cutbacks in government programs and against progressive income tax — did not constitute a majority of the delegates. Thus, only 29% favored a flat tax of 20%, and a plurality of delegates rejected this roll-back philosophy. By 48% to 42%, the delegates said no to cutting welfare to reduce the deficit, and by 51% to 40% they similarly opposed cuts in unemployment insurance to achieve the same objective.[2]

Issue Stands **Conservative Convention, 1983**	% of Conservative Delegates			
	For	Against	No opinion	Net Difference
SOCIAL WELFARE ISSUES				
Means tests for social programs	68	25	7	43
For increasing pensions	54	17	29	37
For allowing extra billing by doctors	41	51	8	10
For cutting back unemployment insurance	40	51	9	11
For reducing deficit by cutting student aid	19	71	10	52
For reducing deficit by cutting back on welfare	42	48	10	6
For greater scrutiny of those receiving unemployment insurance	87	10	3	77

ECONOMIC ISSUES/ GOVERNMENT INTERVENTION IN THE ECONOMY

For more federal government spending for jobs as opposed to leaving that responsibility to private sector	22	71	7	49
Control inflation before employment	36	53	11	17
For more open trade with the US	77	17	6	60
For decreasing the role of FIRA	67	18	15	49
For allowing Canadian oil to rise to world level	51	41	8	10
No strings attached to foreign investment	47	46	7	1
For establishing a 20% flat tax	29	41	30	12

FOREIGN AID

Reduce deficit by cutting foreign aid	64	29	7	35

DEFENSE

For increasing defense spending	72	24	4	48
Increasing Canada's role in NATO	68	23	9	45
For testing the cruise missile	74	21	5	53
Revert armed forces to army, navy, and air force	60	29	11	31

FEDERAL-PROVINCIAL POWERS

For more power to provincial governments	54	17	29	37

LANGUAGE RIGHTS

For increased spending on bilingualism	25	72	3	47

Issue Stands Conservative Convention, 1983	% of Conservative Delegates			
	For	Against	No opinion	Net Difference
BIG GOVERNMENT				
Cut personal taxes even if cuts in government services	55	33	12	22
Reduce corporate taxes and cut services	47	42	11	5
For parliamentary reform	79	10	11	69
For a balanced budget law	24	67	9	43
CROWN CORPORATIONS				
For more government scrutiny of Crown corporations	73	19	8	54
For selling Petro-Canada	61	30	9	31
IMMIGRATION				
For tightening immigration restrictions	67	29	4	38
ABORTION				
For abortion on demand	36	50	14	14
LAW AND ORDER				
For capital punishment	80	17	3	63
For mandatory 10-year sentence for rape	69	20	11	49
Increase spending to create safer streets	51	25	24	26
Independence of the RCMP National Security Service	23	69	8	46
METRIC CONVERSION				
For voluntary metrification	69	25	6	44
CROW RATE				
For changing the Crow rate	46	30	24	16

Table I

QUEBEC'S RED TORIES

This strong Conservative consensus was shared equally by all regions and age groups in the party, save one. French-speaking Conservatives were far more inclined to adopt moderate positions on social and foreign-policy issues than their English-speaking colleagues. While 41% of English-speaking Tories wanted to move the party to the right, only 26% of French-speaking Conservatives shared this wish. Only 3% of English-speaking Tories wanted to move the party to the left (the romantic Red Tory fringe so beloved by Canadian commentators), but 11% of French-speaking Tories wished to see the party move further left. In fact, if there is any Red Tory element left at all in the Progressive Conservative party, it is to be found in Quebec.

The linguistic split on ideology was reflected in several issue stands. For example, 86% of Western Tories favored testing the cruise missile, with 49% of the Quebec delegates opposed; 83% of English-speaking delegates wanted to increase defense spending, but 65% of French-speaking delegates were opposed. Among French-speaking Tories 63% wanted to increase spending on bilingualism, but 81% of English-speaking delegates were opposed; 54% of French-speaking delegates favored compulsory metrification, but 75% of English-speaking Tories were opposed. What is striking is that the only group registering a significant dissent from the overall right-of-center consensus in the Conservative party were French-speaking Tories — perhaps because so many French-speaking delegates to the 1984 convention were recently recruited to the party through the Mulroney-Clark wars.

THE LIBERAL PARTY: THE PARTY OF THE CENTER-LEFT

The Liberal party, as measured by the views on specific issues of party delegates at the 1984 leadership convention, is a party of the center-left. What distinguishes the Liberal party from the Conservative party is that Liberals are much more firmly committed to maintenance of the social safety net and the role that government plays in caring for society's underprivileged. They are more accepting of big government and the services and benefits it provides to society and the individual. They are firm believers in a strong central government. They place more trust in government than in business to act in society's best interest and they advocate a larger, more interventionist role for government in directing the economy and distributing wealth in society. They are stronger proponents of economic self-determination for Canada; and they are more supportive of minority rights. They do not consider defense spending or military strength a priority for Canada. They advocate a less repressive and more rehabilitative approach to law enforcement.

Pierre Trudeau's concept of a Just Society is still, in many respects, at the heart of Liberal political ideology. In reality, the positioning of this ideology is left of center, a positioning which continues to drive the Liberal belief system. It was this ideological stance that attracted the crux of the Liberal coalition, made up of women, youth, the ethnic population and the less fortunate. Liberals believe that a fundamental role of government is to create greater opportunity, and more equal opportunity for all Canadians to share in the wealth of Canada.

Trudeau argued against the granting of any form of special status to any Canadian; he viewed the granting of special status as a form of isolationism. He argued against the granting of special status not as a preservative of distinct culture, but as an inhibitor of opportunity and growth. He wanted all Canadians to have equal opportunities in Canada, in either official language.

Overall, policy consensus in the Liberal party is more uniform than it is in the Conservative party. In surveying 35 issues among Liberal delegates, policy consensus emerged in almost every area with virtually no distinctions among the different sexes or age groups. Some regional patterns of variance were present, but only in a minor key. Most Liberals from all regions, ages and sexes believed in a strong central government, in defending the social safety net and the welfare state and in protection for minorities. Dissenters on these issues did not emerge in any particular region or age category.

The ideological positioning of the Liberal party was clearly evident in the following delegate survey responses: on social-welfare issues, a solid majority of Liberal delegates were against cutting unemployment insurance to reduce the deficit (71% opposed),

72% opposed cutting welfare to reduce the deficit, 83% opposed cutting student aid to reduce the deficit and 62% were against applying means tests for social programs such as family-allowance benefits. In addition, a solid majority of Liberal delegates expressed support for increasing pensions (74% in favor), prohibiting extra billing by doctors (83% in favor) and a guaranteed annual increase (65% in favor).

On economic issues and government intervention in the economy, a solid majority of Liberal delegates expressed support for the federal government's spending more on creating jobs (72% in favor); 67% supported an increase in government grants to industry to create jobs; 78% were in favor of focussing more on creating employment than reducing the deficit. In addition, by a margin of 51% to 41%, Liberal delegates favored more government involvement in creating jobs as opposed to leaving that responsibility to the private sector. There was also no great desire to see the role and size of government cut: 65% opposed reducing taxes if it meant reducing government services.

Regarding federal/provincial powers, the overwhelming majority of Liberal delegates (78%) expressed support for maintaining a strong central government, as opposed to delegating more power to the provinces.

Defense was clearly not a high priority for the Liberal party, as half the delegates interviewed were of the opinion that defense spending should not be increased and a similar proportion felt that Canada's role in NATO should not be increased.

As regards minority rights, immigration, and law and order, Liberal delegates expressed much higher levels of support than Conservative delegates. For increasing spending to encourage bilingualism in Canada (44% of Liberals favored versus 25% of Conservatives); **not** imposing tighter restrictions on immigration (60% of Liberals in favor versus 29% of Conservatives); and, while an overwhelming majority of Conservative delegates (81%) favored a return to capital punishment for some crimes, 42% of Liberals opposed the idea. In addition, a solid majority (90%) of Liberal delegates expressed support for promoting greater equality in women's salaries and 63% favored federal-government intervention over provincial objections to ensure minority language rights. By a margin of 58% to 32% in the West, 64% to 31% in

Ontario, 72% to 20% in Quebec and 55% to 35% in the Atlantic provinces, Liberals rejected John Turner's contention that provinces should have autonomy in deciding language policy.

Issues of greatest consensus among the Liberal delegates were:
*increasing seniors' pensions;
*no extra billing;
*pay equity;
*job creation;
*increased federal power;
*federal strength in federal-provincial confrontation.

The areas of policy dissension within the Liberal party revolved around free trade, Canada's policy with respect to Crown corporations and deficit reduction. Thus, 46% of the delegates wanted more open trade with the U.S., with 47% opposed. Regional variations were striking on this issue: 56% of Western Liberals favored more open trade, while 56% of Ontario Grits and 50% of Quebeckers were opposed. On the matter of financial assistance to Canadair and deHavilland, Western Liberals also differed in opinion from their central-Canadian colleagues: 57% in the West were against assistance compared to 52% in favor in Ontario. The deficit-reduction issue also plainly split the Liberal party, with 51% believing it to be a priority and 46% rejecting it as a critical concern. This division over free trade, deficit reduction and policy regarding Crown corporations was to test the ability of John Turner to develop a coherent party position on these economic issues. But if the Liberals were divided over these issues, they were clearly united on most other policy positions. Liberals not only want to defend the welfare state and social safety net, they wanted to expand it: 74% favored increasing pensions; and 65% favored the introduction of a guaranteed annual income. And while a majority of Liberals have generally favored a reduction of the deficit, by a margin of two or three to one they rejected any proposition to cut services or raise taxes to achieve that goal.[3]

Issue Stands Liberal Convention, 1984	% of Liberal Delegates			
	For	Against	No opinion	Net Difference
SOCIAL WELFARE ISSUES				
For the application of a means test for social programs like family allowances	35	62	3	27
Increase pensions to senior citizens	74	20	6	54
For allowing doctors to extra bill	13	83	4	70
Cut unemployment insurance to reduce deficit	24	71	5	47
For reducing deficit by cutting student aid	12	83	5	47
Cut welfare to reduce deficit	22	72	6	50
For promoting greater equality in women's salaries	90	8	2	82
For a guaranteed annual income	65	28	7	37
Universal daycare for all who require it	43	52	5	9
For compulsory retirement at 65	28	69	3	41

Issue Stands Liberal Convention, 1984	% of Liberal Delegates			
	For	Against	No opinion	Net Differ- ence
ECONOMIC ISSUES/ GOVERNMENT INTERVEN- TION IN THE ECONOMY				
For federal government spending more to create jobs	62	32	6	30
For controlling inflation first before dealing with unemploy- ment	23	70	7	47
For increased open trade with the U.S.	46	47	7	1
Priority for employment over reducing deficit	17	78	5	61
For raising taxes to reduce the deficit	32	63	5	31
For mortgage interest deductibility	62	30	8	32
For decreasing the deficit as a critical issue	51	46	3	5
FOREIGN AID				
For reducing the deficit by cut- ting foreign aid	33	61	6	28
DEFENSE				
For increased spending on defense	43	52	5	9
For increasing Canada's role in NATO	43	50	7	7

FEDERAL-PROVINCIAL POWERS

More power for the federal government	78	12	10	66
For the federal government to take charge in federal-provincial confrontation	75	14	11	61

LANGUAGE RIGHTS

For federal government intervention over provincial objections to ensure minority language rights	63	29	8	34
For increased spending on bi-lingualism	44	53	3	9

BIG GOVERNMENT

Cuts in personal income tax even if it requires a reduction in government services	27	65	8	38
Reduce corporate taxes even if it requires a reduction in government services	23	69	8	46
Increased spending for CBC	13	81	6	68

CROWN CORPORATIONS

For closer government scrutiny of Crown corporations	61	33	6	28
For the federal government to step in financially to save de-Havilland	44	38	18	6
For the federal government to step in financially to save Canadair	42	46	12	4

Issue Stands Liberal Convention, 1984	% of Liberal Delegates			
	For	Against	No opinion	Net Differ- ence
IMMIGRATION				
For tighter immigration restrictions	35	60	5	25
ABORTION				
For abortion on demand	22	67	11	45
LAW AND ORDER				
For capital punishment	55	42	3	13
THE SENATE				
For abolishing the Senate	24	60	16	36
For an elected Senate	58	33	9	25

Table II

QUEBEC'S BLUE GRITS

An interesting parallel with Conservative party delegates emerged from the data. Like the Conservative party, there was a clear policy consensus within the Liberal party on most issues. But also like the Conservative party, Quebec was the center for any dissent. Put simply, Quebec Conservatives have more Red Tories, Quebec Liberals have more Blue Grits.

On most issues, 5% to 7% more Quebec Liberals leaned toward the Conservative position on various issues surveyed than their colleagues from other regions: 22% of Quebec Liberals wanted to decrease the federal budget compared to 18% in the West and 14% in Ontario; 67% of Quebec Liberals opposed cutbacks in welfare to reduce the deficit, but 25% were in favor compared to 20% in favor in the West and 21% in the Atlantic provinces; 33% of Quebec Liberals wanted cuts in corporate taxes, even if it meant a reduction in services, compared to 17% of Western Liberals. And by a margin of 70%, Quebeckers favored the return of capital punishment compared to just 58% of Ontario Liberals. As these findings indicated, French-speaking Liberals were less enthusiastic about active government than their English-speaking colleagues. This was no doubt a reflection of a disenchantment with, and antipathy toward, the strong socialistic policies of the Parti Québécois government, the high taxes that are Quebec's burden and the more conservative orientation of the Quebec Liberal party.

MOVING APART

The Conservative and Liberal delegates who chose Robert Stanfield and Pierre Trudeau in 1967 and 1968 differed in their views regarding policy orientation, but that difference has since widened considerably. Whatever tactical concessions Canada's two major parties make to public opinion and political necessity, they now believe in very different things. The old joke of Tweedledum and Tweedledee is no longer relevant, if it ever was.

Table III shows how Conservative delegates in 1967 differed from Liberal delegates in 1968.[4] Table IV, based on our two surveys of delegates attending the 1983 and 1984 Conservative and Liberal leadership conventions reveals the differences today.[5] In the 1960s, on issues like medicare and the granting of more power to the provinces, the two parties differed dramatically, but on most issues the index of disagreement (that is, the net difference between the proportion of Liberal delegates and the proportion of Conservative delegates who agree with such policy positions) was 10% or less. In the 1980s, on issues of federal/provincial powers, the index of disagreement was 61% and on many issues the two parties differed by 30% or more. In other words, in the two decades since 1967, they have moved apart radically.

Policy Difference Between the Parties
1967 and 1968 Conservative and Liberal Leadership Conventions.

	% Liberal Delegates Agree	% Conservative Delegates Agree	Net Difference (Index of Disagreement)
Social Welfare Issues			
Free medicare should be available to aged	50	18	32
Old-age pensions and baby bonuses should only be paid to those in need	51	66	15
Governments spend too much on social welfare	47	59	12
Government has a responsibility to help those unable to look after themselves	94	93	1
Economic Issues/Government Intervention In The Economy			
Government should interfere less with business	35	61	26
There should be special laws to regulate foreign (mostly U.S.) capital	66	58	8
More government planning is needed to develop the Canadian economy	79	72	7
The workers' right to strike should not be restricted	27	23	4
Canadian political parties cater too much to farmers	19	16	3
We should seek greater American investment in Canada	55	58	3
More federal spending toward development of economies of poor provinces	87	85	2

Foreign Policy

Canada should bring its foreign policy more closely into line with the U.S.	13	19	6
Soviet communism is no longer a threat to Canada	47	42	5
Canada should donate more aid to the underdeveloped countries	63	52	11
The Commonwealth connection is no longer important for Canada	39	25	14

Defense

Canada should spend less on defense	67	59	8

Federal-Provincial Powers

The federal government should give more money to provinces	30	56	26
Provincial government should have more power	15	33	18

The Monarchy

The monarchy is an essential part of the Canadian Constitution	29	57	28

Language Rights

French-speaking Canadians outside Quebec should be able to use French when dealing with own government	73	58	15

Table III

Liberal delegates in the 1980s remained wedded to social welfare and wanted to expand it. Conservatives wanted to cut back on social welfare and reduce the deficit. Liberals favored the federal

government and distrusted the provinces; Tories favored the provinces and distrusted the federal government. Conservatives
favored an increase in defense spending; Liberals gave military
spending a low priority and favored foreign aid. The two parties
were closer on issues like economic intervention (with one wing of
the Liberal party agreeing with the dominant Conservative position), but even here the two parties, overall, differed widely on
issues relative to the sale of Crown corporations and trade relations with the United States. Moreover, Liberals tended to place
more trust in government than in business and wanted government
to play a bigger role in directing the economy and distributing
wealth in society. Conservatives, on the other hand, trusted
business more than government. They wanted government to play
a smaller role in the economy and to encourage individuals to
become more responsible for their own well-being. They were the
champions of individual initiative and self-reliance, with Liberals
more sympathetic to minority rights. Conservatives wanted tough
measures to maintain law and order while Liberals were the civil
libertarians. Liberals supported active, participatory strong
federalism; Conservatives favored passive, adjudicative and weak
federalism.

Policy Difference Between the Parties
1983 and 1984 Conservative and Liberal Leadership Conventions.

	% Liberal Delegates Agree	% Conservative Delegates Agree	Net Difference (Index of Disagreement)
Social Welfare Issues			
Continuing to allow social programs like family allowances to benefit all Canada equally	62	25	37
Prohibiting extra billing	83	51	32
Oppose cutting back on welfare to reduce the deficit	72	48	24
For increasing pensions to elderly	74	54	20
Oppose cutting back on unemployment insurance to reduce deficit	71	51	20
Oppose cutting student aid to reduce deficit	83	71	12
Economic Issues/Government Intervention In The Economy			
For the federal government's spending more money to create jobs	51	22	29
For increased open trade with U.S.	46	77	31
Deal with unemployment ahead of inflation	70	53	17
Foreign Policy			
Not cutting back on foreign aid to reduce the deficit	61	29	32

Policy Difference Between the Parties
1983 and 1984 Conservative and Liberal Leadership Conventions.

	% Liberal Delegates Agree	% Conservative Delegates Agree	Net Difference (Index of Disagreement)
Defense			
Oppose increasing defense spending	52	24	28
Oppose increasing Canada's role in NATO	50	23	27
Federal-Provincial Powers			
For more power for federal government	78	17	61
Language Rights			
Against increased spending on bilingualism	53	72	19
Big Government			
Oppose reducing personal taxes if it meant a reduction in government services	65	33	32
Oppose reducing corporate taxes if it meant a reduction in government services	69	42	27
Crown Corporations			
For closer government scrutiny of Crown corporations	61	73	12
Immigration			
Oppose tighening up on immigration	60	29	31
Abortion			
Favor abortion on demand	22	36	14
Law And Order			
For capital punishment	55	80	25

Table IV

From the 1960s to the 1980s, the Liberal party has dominated in federal electoral contests while the Conservatives have been equally successful provincially. The Liberal party's devotion to federal power was sharpened by savage disagreements with the provinces over the Constitution and energy policy. In this same period, the Liberals introduced medicare, the guaranteed income supplement for the elderly poor and the child tax credit. Spending for social welfare became an article of faith. Defense spending was frozen to pay for these programs and arms control rather than military preparedness became a Liberal passion. Despite the division in the party over American investment, the Trudeau government also created the Foreign Investment Review Agency, the Canada Development Corporation and the National Energy Program. The Liberals became the party of economic nationalism, even though a significant wing of the party was always uneasy about these initiatives. In the 16 years between the two Liberal leadership conventions, the Liberal party became more liberal on social policy, even firmer in its devotion to a strong central government and more activist and nationalistic on economic questions, especially foreign investment. As Canada moved from the affluent sixties to the recession of the eighties, the Liberal party stayed liberal or even became a little more progressive or left of center.

This minor shift in Liberal policy values contrasts with a dramatic change in Conservative party beliefs. In the 20 years between the time John Diefenbaker led a Conservative federal government to victory and 1983, the year the party chose Brian Mulroney, the Conservatives became more militant in their approach to the federal government, social welfare, the Soviet threat, and active government intervention in the economy. The new right-wing agenda of American conservatives has entered Canada through the Conservative party, just as the New Deal and Great Society liberal activism of the 1960s was adopted by the Liberal party of Canada. The Conservative party moved to the right while the Liberal party remained wedded to the activist social-welfare agenda of the 1960s. John Turner and Brian Mulroney may have resembled one another in background, philosophy and approach, but the two parties they led were now very, very different.

CHANGING PLACES

The two major parties of Canada not only have moved apart since the 1960s, but they also have assumed each others' historical clothes. The values of the Liberal party activists began to approximate the policy traditions of Sir John A. Macdonald's brand of conservatism, while the modern Conservative party became a rigorous proponent of nineteenth-century liberalism.

This trend began in the 1960s. While on average there was only a 10% difference between the priorities of Liberal and Conservative activists, the Liberals leaned toward a more dynamic centralist government: as Table III indicates, 50% of Liberals favored medicare compared to 18% for the Conservatives; 61% of the Conservatives wanted government to interfere less with business compared to 35% of Liberal delegates; and twice as many Conservatives as Liberals — 33% to 15% — wanted to give the provinces more power. The historical legacy of Macdonald within the Conservative party was reflected primarily in the greater dedication of Tories to British traditions; thus, 57% of Conservatives believed the monarchy to be essential compared to 29% of the Liberals. The Liberals also were far more skeptical of the Commonwealth, with 39% no longer deeming that institution important.

Evident even in the 1960s, this divergence intensified in subsequent years. As Table IV demonstrates, by the mid-1980s Liberal and Conservative activists differed by 20 to 30% on most issues. The fault lines were most apparent on issues that Sir John A. Macdonald would have recognized: 77% of the Conservatives wanted open trade with the United States and only 46% of Liberals agreed; 78% of Liberal activists wanted more power for the federal government compared to only 17% of the Tories. By wide margins, Liberals also were more opposed to cutting back on unemployment insurance, welfare and foreign aid to reduce the deficit. Sixty-five percent of Liberals, for example, nearly twice as many as in the Conservative camp, opposed reducing personal income taxes if government services would suffer.

Yet if Conservatives in the 1960s retained affection for the British Crown, their successors in the 1980s also remained true to another part of the Conservative legacy — the need for strong military forces. The Conservatives have traditionally been the party of "Ready, aye ready" and this tradition continues. If the Liberals are the party of social welfare, the Tories are the party of military readiness: in the 1983–84 conventions, 52% of Liberals opposed increasing defense spending, but only 24% of Conservatives were similarly dovish. Most Tories wanted to increase Canada's role in NATO, while most Liberals were opposed. Although they adopted the laissez-faire perspective of nineteenth-century liberalism regarding the economy, the modern Canadian Conservative party had no equivalent affection for the anti-military, non-interventionist values of Gladstone, Cobden and Bright.

The values of our two major parties diverge radically and their ideological stance has been transformed: the Liberals are now the party of centralism, nationalism and activism, while Conservatives defend Laurier's truths of provincial rights, limited government and close relations with the United States. The Liberal and Conservative parties have not only moved apart — they have changed places.

6

Marching To a Different Drummer

Not only did the Liberal and Conservative parties occupy different ends of the political spectrum as measured by the beliefs of each party's delegates, but the constituency of voters each party traditionally attracted reflects also the differences in each party's political ideology.

When one examines who traditionally has voted Liberal and who traditionally has voted Conservative in this country, one finds that the core of the Liberal party's support has come from ethnic and minority Canadians, French-Canadians, women, young people and middle to lower-income earners.

In other words, the traditional core of the Liberal party's base of support in this country has been Canadians who are middle to lower class and a coalition of minority groups — Canadians who have had to struggle in recent years to make ends meet. These people are not affluent. They do not have a great deal of financial, economic or job security. These are the people most likely to have been frustrated by a lack of opportunity to get ahead in society or to have experienced discrimination of one form or another due to their socio-economic status and minority status. They are also the people most likely to need and benefit from government social services or assistance programs and the social safety net that government can provide.

What all these people who make up the core of the Liberal party's traditional constituency share, to varying degrees, is a sense of vulnerability. And they look to government to help reduce their sense of vulnerability.

Conservative party support, on the other hand, traditionally has come from upper-middle-class Canadians or upwardly mobile Canadians, males and older Canadians.

In short, the "haves" constitute the traditional Conservative supporters and the "have less" make up traditional Liberal support.

Delegate surveys revealed that each party's delegates clearly had a good sense of whence came their party's support and who made up their traditional constituency of voters. The left-of-center, social-welfare ideology of the Liberal party delegates evolved from a grassroots level and reflected the socio-economic makeup of the Liberal party's traditional core constituency. The political ideology articulated by the Liberal party delegates had the popular support of the Liberal party's grassroots constituency of traditional supporters: people who felt vulnerable because of their socio-economic status. They were attracted to the left-of-center social-welfare ideology of the Liberal party because they found security in it and viewed it as serving their own self-interest. They were committed to maintaining the social safety net and the social services that government provided because this reduced their sense of vulnerability. They looked to government to play an active role in the economy in order to create greater equality of opportunity for people like themselves.

The right-of-center ideology of the Conservative party delegates was similarly reflected and the value structure of the party's ideology was rooted in the value structure of upper-middle-class and upwardly mobile Canadians. These were the people who believed most fervently in the tenets of the free-market system, individual initiative and self-reliance at the heart of the Conservative party ideology.

At the same time that we collected data among Liberal and Conservative convention delegates, we surveyed grassroots or core supporters of both parties. Tables I and II illustrate how the same right/left ideological orientation already observed in the delegate convention survey data was also evident among the grassroots supporters of the Conservative and Liberal parties.

Core supporters of the Liberal party, that is those who considered themselves to be Liberals, were clearly more left of center in their ideology than voters who considered themselves to be Conservatives. More specifically, those who considered themselves Liberal were much more inclined than those who identified themselves as Conservative to favor more federal spending on job creation. They were against cutting back on student aid, welfare and unemployment insurance to reduce the deficit. They were against increasing defense spending. They were for a strong central government and a guaranteed income program.

Conservative party supporters, on the other hand, exhibited relatively more right-wing views. They were, for example, much more inclined to favor capital punishment, to agree with reducing the federal deficit by cutting back on welfare, unemployment insurance and foreign aid, to favor making Crown corporations financially self-supporting, and to favor increased defense spending. They were in favor of granting more power to the provinces and were against increased spending on bilingualism programs.

Although generally the delegates' views and values reflect those of the parties' supporters, in both Conservative and Liberal camps there were some areas of dissonance.

Liberal delegates and supporters, for example, demonstrated the same viewpoints regarding free trade, extra billing, job creation, fiscal responsiblity and Canada's role in NATO. However, areas of some dissonance included:

> –federal/provincial responsibilities (78% of delegates
> and 45% of supporters advocated more power for the
> federal government and a strong central government;
> 75% of delegates and 48% of supporters opted for a
> stronger, central government where the federal govern-
> ment would take charge when federal/provincial con-
> frontation occurs; while 63% of delegates and 39% of
> supporters were in favor of federal intervention over
> provincial objections in the assurance of minority
> language rights);
> –foreign affairs (35% of delegates, but 65% of supporters
> were in favor of the imposition of tighter immigration
> restrictions; 33% of delegates and 59% of supporters
> opted for a reduction of the federal deficit by a cutback
> in foreign aid; 23% of delegates and 51% of supporters
> favored increasing the value of the Canadian dollar
> closer to that of the American dollar);
> –means tests for social programs (35% of delegates and
> 64% of supporters favored the application of a means
> test for social programs such as family allowances).

In other words, on these issues delegates tended to be more federalist and slightly to the left of supporters.[1]

Preferred Stance On The Issues	% of Respondents	
	Liberal delegates	Liberal supporters
Moral Issues:		
For capital punishment under certain circumstances	55	68
Against capital punishment under any circumstances	42	27
For allowing Canadians to retire earlier, for example at 55	40	46
For leaving retirement policy as it exists	55	49
For instituting compulsory retirement at age 65	28	39
For allowing people to decide on their own at what age they should retire	69	59
For abortion on demand	22	36
For keeping abortion policy as it exists	67	56
Social Welfare Issues:		
For promoting greater equality in women's salaries	90	83
Not doing anything further in that regard	8	14
For increasing pensions to older people	74	86
For maintaining pensions as they are now	20	5
For a guaranteed income for needy Canadians	65	78

	% of Respondents	
Preferred Stance On The Issues	Liberal delegates	Liberal supporters
Not for any form of guaranteed income	28	16
For the availability of day-care services for everyone who requires them	43	53
For some restrictions as to the availability of day-care	52	42
For the application of means tests for social programs such as family allowance benefits	35	64
For continuing to allow such programs to benefit all Canadians equally	62	32
For reducing personal income taxes requiring an attendant cut in government services	27	46
Not reducing taxes and leaving government services at present levels	65	47
For allowing extra billing by doctors and hospitals	13	14
For prohibiting extra billing	83	82
Federal Deficit/Taxation/Government Services:		
For revision of the tax system to encourage more investment by private industry	84	79
Not for such reform	11	11
For some type of mortgage relief such as an interest rate subsidy on mortgage interest deductibility	61	59
Not for providing mortgage interest relief, allowing market forces to prevail	30	34

Preferred Stance On The Issues	% of Respondents	
	Liberal delegates	Liberal supporters
For decreasing the federal deficit	51	57
Not a critical issue in your mind	46	39
For lower interest rates, even if it means a lower Canadian dollar relative to the U.S. dollar	49	49
For Canadian dollar stability relative to the U.S. dollar, at the expense of higher interest rates, if necessary	41	42
For legislative control of interest rates	36	51
For allowing interest rates to rise and fall with the economy	59	44
For reducing the federal deficit by cutting back on foreign aid	33	59
Not cutting back on foreign aid to reduce the deficit	61	36
For raising taxes to reduce the federal deficit	32	25
Not raising taxes to reduce the deficit	63	71
For reducing the federal deficit by cutting back on unemployment insurance benefits	24	33
Not cutting back on unemployment insurance benefits to reduce the deficit	71	63
For reducing corporate income taxes, requiring an attendant cut in government services	23	38
Not reducing taxes and leaving government services at present levels	69	52
For reducing the federal deficit by cutting back on welfare	22	37

Preferred Stance On The Issues	% of Respondents	
	Liberal delegates	Liberal supporters
Not cutting back on welfare to reduce the deficit	72	59
For focusing more on decreasing the federal budget	17	24
For focusing more on creating employment	78	73
For reducing the federal deficit by cutting student aid	12	20
Not cutting student aid to reduce the deficit	83	75
Job Creation:		
For more government grants to industry to create jobs	67	80
Not putting any more money into job creation	28	18
For the federal government spending more money to create jobs	62	81
Not putting any money into job creation	32	16
For the federal government spending more money to create jobs	51	68
For leaving that responsibility to the private sector	40	28
For the federal government spending more money to create jobs	29	36
For more government grants to industry to create jobs	59	56
For trying to combat inflation in Canada first	23	23
For trying to deal with Canada's unemployment level first	70	74

Preferred Stance On The Issues	% of Respondents	
	Liberal delegates	Liberal supporters
Free Trade/Foreign Affairs/ Immigration:		
For increased open trade with the United States	46	49
For maintaining the current trade level	47	45
For increasing Canada's role in NATO	43	40
Not increasing Canada's role in NATO	50	48
For increasing Canada's defense spending	43	35
Not increasing defense spending	52	60
For imposing tighter immigration restrictions	35	65
Leaving immigration policy as it exists today	60	29
For increasing the value of the Canadian dollar closer to that of the American dollar	23	51
For allowing the value of the Canadian dollar to float naturally relative to the U.S. dollar	71	42
Crown Corporations/Privatization:		
For closer government involvement in and more scrutiny of Crown corporations	61	49
For allowing Crown corporations to function with less government involvement	33	39

Preferred Stance On The Issues	% of Respondents	
	Liberal delegates	Liberal supporters
For the federal government stepping in financially to save deHavilland	44	27
For making deHavilland survive or not on its own	39	41
For the federal government stepping in financially to save Canadair	42	35
For making Canadair survive or not on its own	46	57
For more money to be provided the CBC for development and expansion	13	15
For maintaining current levels of support for the CBC	81	78
Federalism/Parliamentary Reform:		
For more power for the federal government and a strong central government	78	45
For more power for the provincial governments	12	40
For a stronger central government where the federal government takes charge where federal-provincial confrontation occurs	75	48
For more power for provincial governments and more autonomy for them to act on their own when confrontation develops	14	42
For federal government intervention over provincial objections in the assurance of minority language rights	63	39
For minority language rights to be more of a provincial matter	29	51

For increased spending to encourage bilingualism in Canada	44	30
Not considering increased spending on bilingualism	53	63
For maintaining the Senate	33	26
For an elected Senate	58	57
For abolishing the Senate	24	40
For maintaining the Senate as it is	60	45

Table I

For the Conservatives, however, party supporters were to the left of delegates on several issues. While there was clear consensus in many areas — attitudes toward capital punishment, abortion, a means test for social programs, taxation, foreign aid, bilingualism, immigration and fiscal responsibility among them — delegates tended to be further to the right than supporters in terms of:

— free trade (77% of delegates and 54% of supporters favored increased open trade with the U.S.);

— defense (75% of delegates and 42% of supporters sanctioned increased defense spending);

— job creation (71% of delegates and 38% of supporters felt that job creation should be the responsibility of the private sector);

— social welfare (54% of delegates and 90% of supporters favored increasing pensions; 42% of delegates and 20% of supporters supported extra billing; 55% of delegates and 36% of supporters were in favor of a reduction in personal income taxes with an attendant cut in government services).[2]

Preferred Stance On The Issues	% of Respondents	
	Conservative delegates	Conservative supporters
Moral Issues:		
For capital punishment under certain circumstances	81	80
Or not	17	16
For abortion on demand	36	38
Or not	50	54
Social Welfare Issues:		
For the application of means tests for social programs such as family allowance	68	71
Or not	25	27
For increasing pensions	54	90
For decreasing pensions in order to reduce the federal deficit	43	6
For allowing extra billing by doctors and hospitals	42	20
Or not	51	77
Federal Deficit/Taxation/ Government Services:		
For reducing the federal deficit by cutting back on foreign aid	64	66
Or not	29	27
For reducing personal income taxes requiring an attendant cut in government services	55	36
Or not	33	54
For reducing corporate income taxes, requiring an attendant cut in government services	47	49
Or not	42	45

For reducing the federal deficit by cutting back on welfare	42	41
Or not	48	53
For reducing the federal deficit by cutting back on unemployment insurance	40	39
Or not	51	56
For legislative control of interest rates	36	41
Or not	57	52
For reducing the federal deficit by cutting student aid	19	33
Or not	71	63
Job Creation:		
For trying to combat inflation in Canada first	36	29
For trying to deal with Canada's unemployment level first	53	67
For the federal government spending more money to create jobs	22	59
For leaving that responsibility to the private sector	71	38
Free Trade/Foreign Affairs/ Immigration:		
For increased open trade with the United States, that is, decreased trade barriers	77	54
Or not	17	41
For increasing Canada's defense spending	72	42
Or not	24	55
For increasing Canada's role in NATO	68	51
Or not	23	40

Preferred Stance On The Issues	% of Respondents	
	Conservative delegates	Conservative supporters
For imposing tighter immigration restrictions	67	65
Or not	29	31
For increasing the value of the Canadian dollar closer to that of the American dollar	46	45
Or not	40	50
Crown Corporations:		
For more government involvement in and scrutiny of Crown corporations	73	55
Or not	19	39
Federalism:		
For increased spending to promote bilingualism	25	19
Or not	72	77
For more power for the federal government	17	26
For more power for the provincial governments	54	62

Table II

Despite assertions to the contrary, the electorate does, in fact, distinguish between the political ideology of the Liberal and Conservative parties. There is a sense that the Liberal and Conservative parties do differ in their political orientation and ideology. Voters have tended to gravitate to a party based on their perception of what the party stands for and to gravitate to the party whose value or belief structure is closest to their own.

Self-serving overall, voters have tended to vote for the party they viewed as most capable of improving their personal circumstances.

The questions any party must address — questions that will decide the destiny of any party in any election — are simple: (1) where is the economy of the country headed, and (2) what impact will it have in terms of the "haves" and "have nots." Voter turnaround and voter optimism is never independent of the perceived promise of economic well-being, even relative to short-term economic positioning. Political orientation is a function of voter perception of a party's performance in the economic arena. Voters tend to vote with their stomachs and out of economic self-interest.

Contained within that self-interest is also a strong degree of economic nationalism. People vote with more than just their pocketbook: public opinion consistently demonstrates a trepidation at the prospect of losing sovereignty through the loss of economic independence.

Political parties are driven by a commitment to a particular value system and the desire to win. While it has been demonstrated that delegates are consistent in their beliefs, the party leadership can steer a party ideologically to the right or left as part of a strategy to gain public favor. The tables illustrating activist versus grassroots perspectives regarding policy position reflect the shifting leadership-activist-grassroots triumvirate.

The push and pull of ideology versus winnability, the role of the leadership and public opinion and issues relative to Canadian sovereignty and economic independence all became core factors in the dramatic events which swept Canadian political life in the second half of the 1980s.

PART TWO
TOWARD A
FEDERAL ELECTION

7

1986: Turner Reviewed

The Liberals who met at the Ottawa Convention Centre in late November 1986, were sadder but wiser. Two years earlier, they had bartered their collective political and ideological soul for winnability and lost — resoundingly. Not only had they compromised Liberal values and policy orientation, they also had misinterpreted the mood of the public, a public which had in 1984 voted against a Liberal party perceived to be farther to the right than tradition and national understanding would have it. The delegates at the 1984 convention had been out of step with the public. The electorate felt that the party had moved too far to the right under Turner and vacated its traditional left-of-center position.

Two years later the Liberal delegation to the 1986 review convention reconfirmed Edmund Burke's two-centuries-old definition of political parties. The convention might have been motivated, and its mood dominated, by factionalism, antagonism and confusion, but it served, if inadvertently, to demonstrate an important and fundamental aspect of liberalism in Canada: the convention demonstrated the Liberals indeed to be ". . . a body of men *(and women) promoting by joint (if at times contestable) endeavors* the national interest *(social welfare, social security, job creation, economic growth through involved government)* upon some particular principle *(centralization, national unity, Canadian sovereignty, strong activist government, peace and disarmament)* in which they are all agreed."

The proof lies in numbers, numbers which were derived from a survey of 600 convention delegates in a poll sponsored conjointly by the *Toronto Star* and the CTV network. The first statistic to which close attention must be drawn, tells us that **more than half** (52%) of the delegates in 1986 had *not been* at the 1984 convention. The important point is not so much that Turner had done a good job sprinkling the grassroots with his own seeds — as

Mulroney, his Conservative mirror-image, had done three years earlier — but that Turner had attracted a whole new group of party activists to the Liberal fold.

More than 1,500 new faces and new voices were brought into the Liberal activist camp. Presumably a healthy percentage of the new delegates supported Turner and his right-of-center, business-oriented interpretation of liberalism. Many of the questions asked in the 1984 poll were intentionally repeated in 1986. Yet a very important aspect of the Liberal value system emerged. The new delegates had not, obviously, participated in the poll taken at the 1984 convention, but when asked to comment in 1986, there were virtually no attitudinal shifts indicated; divergences were at best extremely slight, as Table 1, which compares results for the two conventions for issue-related statements, indicates. First-time delegates upheld the traditional Liberal point of view, as if abiding by an unwritten collective political unconscious.

These new Liberal activists — Turner supporters among them — demonstrated the tenacity and continuity of political orientation that defines liberalism/Liberalism. They continued to define themselves as small *l* liberals who proclaimed traditional Liberal values, regardless of their leader's name, constituency or political orientation.

The delegates in 1986 declared themselves left of center in their stance **on specific issues.** Seventy-eight percent indicated that the government should be focussing more on creating employment than decreasing the federal deficit (17%); 65% supported the idea of a guaranteed income for Canadians; 71% opposed cutting back on unemployment insurance to reduce the deficit; and a similar proportion (71%) opposed cutting back on welfare to reduce the deficit. They also favored strong activist centralist government. For example, 57% were against giving Quebec a veto over constitutional changes and 73% were opposed to free trade.

As Table I indicates, the continuity exhibited by delegates at both conventions is startling.[1] For example, 71% of Liberal delegates at both conventions opposed cutting back on welfare to reduce the deficit. In 1984, 78% of delegates supported focussing more on creating jobs than cutting the deficit as compared to 75% of the 1986 delegates. In 1984, 63% of delegates opposed raising taxes to reduce the deficit as compared with 57% two years later.

	% of 1984 Delegates	% of 1986 Delegates	Net Difference
For a guaranteed income for Canadians	65	65	0
Against cutting back on welfare to reduce the federal deficit	72	71	1
Who feel that decreasing the federal budget deficit is not a critical issue	46	43	3
For focusing on creating employment rather than decreasing the federal budget deficit	75	78	3
For the federal government to spend more money to create jobs	51	55	4
Against raising taxes to reduce the deficit	57	63	6
For not reducing taxes and leaving government services at present levels	58	65	7

TABLE I

The Liberals at this convention clearly upheld traditional Liberal values. If any shift took place between 1984 and 1986, it was a move toward greater fiscal and economic responsibility, but **not** at the expense of social programs. Gray areas, in which consensus was not as great, included the degree to which reduction of the federal deficit was critical, the degree to which foreign business investment in Canada was desirable, the degree of eligibility of UIC payments and the capital-punishment issue.

The issues, however, which elicited the greatest support were still:

* maintaining the amount of money spent on health services to reduce the deficit (87% of delegates)

* lowering tariff barriers only in selected areas, rather than the removal of all trade barriers (76% of delegates)
* focussing on creating employment, rather than on reducing the federal budget deficit (75% of delegates)

The electorate had perceived in 1984 that the two major parties were moving closer together. In fact, they were not. Conservatives and Liberals both maintained distinctive value systems and attitudes, as the following table indicates, about four issues (free trade, job creation, capital punishment and government services).[2]

	% of 1984 Liberal Delegates	% of 1986 Liberal Delegates	% of 1983 Conservative Delegates
For increasing open trade with the U.S.	46	20	77
For reducing personal income taxes with an attendant cut in government services	27	33	55
Against capital punishment	42	48	17
Against the government's spending money to create jobs and for leaving that responsibility to the private sector	40	30	71

TABLE II

Another fundamental difference in orientation between the two parties was their variant perceptions of the role of an activist government. Conservative government is passive, laissez-faire government: Conservatives adjudicate rather than activate. Liberals view government's role as an active one — to stimulate, to encourage and to get involved.

The 70 resolutions passed at the 1986 convention reflected traditional Liberal viewpoints. Priority was given to aboriginal-rights issues, northern and regional development, the environment and arms control, international cooperation, education and social welfare issues, such as aging, child care, housing, guaranteed income, women's rights and so forth. (One area of dissension or split policy was with respect to free trade and economic nationalism.)

Resolution 11, for example, resolved that "Canada pursue its role as a leader in world peace and disarmament by seeking a multilateral verifiable disarmament treaty together with a policy of non-interference by super powers in the internal affairs of other nations." Resolution 22 proposed the establishment of a six-month task force on aging, a national conference devoted to this subject and the creation of a ministry of aging. Resolution 48 proposed a universal income-support program in view of the "strong tradition of caring and sharing" (of the Liberal party). Resolution 67 resolved "that the Liberal party of Canada reaffirm its intention to pursue, when re-elected, an independent foreign policy giving priority to the interests of Canada, world peace and the sharing of resources."[3]

When delegates were asked to place themselves and their party on a one-to-ten ideological scale, however (where a "one" indicated the far left and a "ten" the far right), a slight ideological schizophrenia began to emerge. Liberal delegates placed the Liberal party at 5.5 on the scale (further right than the post-Trudeau 1984 position of 5.2), themselves at 5.3 and John Turner at 5.9. That is, Liberal delegates viewed John Turner as still being both further to the right than the party should have been and further to the right than they themselves were. When we compare these findings with those of 1984, we see that delegates indicated their perception of a very slight shift to the left for John Turner (-.3) and for the Conservatives (-.2), but that they viewed the Liberal party itself in 1986 as further right than it had been in 1984 by + .3 degrees, as Table III shows.[4]

Where A "1" Represents The Political Left, And A "10" Represents The Right,	% of Delegates		Index of Difference
	1984 Liberals	1986 Liberals	
You are	5.4	5.3	-.1
The Conservative party is	6.7	6.5	-.2
John Turner is	6.2	5.9	-.3
The Liberal party is	5.2	5.5	+.3

Table III

The fact that Liberals placed themselves at 5.5 on the political scale, yet were decidedly left of center in policy stances was indicative of confusion — an identity crisis of sorts — within the party. This confusion was to haunt the party in the subsequent 12 months.

The shift in ideological self-identification from the post-Trudeau 1984 convention at 5.2 to 5.5 in 1986 clearly demonstrates the reciprocity thesis presented in the opening chapter: that a party is an active mix of leadership, activists and grassroots supporters. The ideological shift reflects Turner's influence on the party while at the same time, the data gathered at the 1986 convention — particularly in terms of foreign investment, sales tax for business and so forth — demonstrate the influence of the activists on Turner himself, a shift further confirmed by the positioning of Turner at 6.2 in 1984 and 5.9 two years later.

Liberals placed themselves marginally closer to the Conservatives, but consistently voted Liberal in policy terms. Like the American Republicans, they were being "operationally Liberal" in taking an ideological stance further right than their policy perspectives. Liberals identified themselves as marginally right of center, but in terms of policy positions were traditionally Liberal.

Policies endorsed by the Liberals clearly are suggestive of a party who presumably would rank itself most strongly at a 4 or 5 on the ideological scale. However, if one examines the breakdown of individual percentages for 4, 5 and 6 in Table IV, this is clearly not the case: 53% of Liberals gave themselves a 4 or a 5, but only 47% identified their party accordingly.[5]

Ideological Positioning ('1' = Far Left '10' = Far Right	% of Liberal delegates					
	The Liberal Party	Self	John Turner	The Conser- vative Party	Brian Mulroney	The NDP
(1-3)	(3)	(9)	(4)	(9)	(11)	(50)
4	19	21	9	7	6	24
5	28	32	32	11	13	13
6	25	16	24	14	18	3
(7-10)	(21)	(20)	(28)	(56)	(46)	(5)
Average Ranking	5.5	5.3	5.9	6.5	6.3	3.6

Table IV

When asked directly if the Liberal party's overall stance should remain as it was or be more to the right or the left, 53% supported the view that the party should stay where it was, 29% supported a move to the left and only 12% endorsed a move to the right. Clearly, the party, and John Turner himself, were viewed as too far right for comfort.

This sentiment was also evident in delegate perceptions about where John Turner stood on some specific issues, such as the deficit, compared to their own viewpoints. Delegates were asked, on a number of issues, to rank their own views and those of Turner on a 10-point scale, in which a 1 indicated strong opposition, and a 10 indicated strong support. On the issue of decreasing the deficit, delegates placed themselves at 6.1 and John Turner at 6.6: Liberal delegates still viewed John Turner as being significantly further to the right than they on the deficit issue.[6]

Noteworthy differences were revealed in Turner's perceived position and the position of the Liberal delegates on other issues as well. In particular, Liberal delegates saw Turner as being much more supportive of free trade (support index: 5.0 for Turner versus 4.1 for the delegates) and, harbinger of things to come, as being more supportive of giving Quebec a constitutional veto than they were (support index: 6.5 for Turner versus 4.7 for the delegates). The delegates elected Turner as their leader, but were not wholly prepared to follow his guidance when it was inspired by his personal instincts about philosophical values. While the problems created by the Meech Lake Accord were to come later, the data here — the ideological shift — showed the potential for discord, as disparity was perceived particularly in areas relative to federal/provincial relations.

Where Do You Stand And Where Do You Think John Turner Stands On The Following Issues? *(where a "1" indicates strong opposition and a "10" strong support)*	Self-Identification	John Turner	Index of Difference
AREAS IN WHICH TURNER FELT TO DEMONSTRATE GREATER SUPPORT:			
Giving Quebec a veto over constitutional changes to bring Quebec into the constitution	4.7	6.5	2.2
Free trade with the U.S.	4.1	5.0	0.9
Focusing on decreasing the federal deficit	6.1	6.6	0.5
For lowering tariff barriers in selected areas with the U.S.	6.4	6.8	0.4
AREAS IN WHICH TURNER FELT TO DEMONSTRATE WEAKER SUPPORT:			
Reducing the barriers to interprovincial trade	8.0	7.6	-0.4
Reform of the Senate to make it an elected body	6.5	6.1	-0.4

TABLE V

Given, then, the fundamental entrenchment of Liberal values demonstrated at the two conventions and the slight disparity in perspectives held by the leader as opposed to party activists, what was it that eventually catapulted the party into the soul-wrenching, costly and divisive exercise that was the 1986 convention? The 1986 leadership convention was primarily about leadership. It was also about the role of a leader within the party and about policy continuity and ideology. When questioned about the key issues facing them, 59% of the delegates made mention of the leadership review issue, but 35% also made reference to the need to develop *clear* policy positions and a consensus of *direction* for the party. While it was about leadership, the major themes which emerged from the convention had implications far beyond leadership itself.

The convention demonstrated:

* the tenacity and continuity of Liberal values and policy;
* an ideological conflict, which sowed the seeds for potential future discord;
* the interactive relationship between leader and party;
* the role of the convention process itself in creating a leader;
* the role of the old guard;
* the issue of winnability.

In round two, as in round one, John Turner was victorious. Support ultimately remained with the party leader. The results of the poll indicated that 78% of delegates were against a leadership review and 22% in favor. (In fact, by the final count, 76.3% of delegates re-endorsed Turner's leadership.) The key factor in the vote *for* review was winnability, although for left-of-center Liberals, Turner's stand on issues was identified as carrying some importance.

When delegates were asked to distribute 10 points among four factors — leadership, personality, winnability and stand on issues — in ranking desirable qualities in a leader, results were distributed as follows:

Leadership ability 3.0
Stand on issues 2.9
Ability to win 2.5
Personality 2.0[7]

During the fall of 1986 Turner was ahead in the polls for the first and only time since 1984. Two months later, the NDP began to rise, and within several months actually surpassed the Liberals. The Liberals, however, had already banked on Turner and possible winnability. In this sense, the convention process itself, spurred on by poll results and media coverage, vaulted Turner forward.

Four of five delegates had voted against a leadership review and identified their reasons as follows in Table VI. Greatest support came from Quebec delegates and right-of-center Liberals.[8]

Why Are You Voting Against A Leadership Review?	% of Delegates who voted against leadership review				
	TOTAL	QUEBEC	IDEOLOGICAL POSITION		
			Left	Right	Center
Because Turner deserves a chance/another chance to prove his leadership	23	19	22	23	24
Have confidence in Turner's leadership ability	22	23	22	22	24
Because Turner can win the next election	19	29	11	23	19
Feel there is no one else available who would make a better leader	15	23	14	18	11
Have confidence in Turner's personality/public image/appeal	12	21	9	12	15
Feel a leadership convention would hurt the party at this time	12	20	10	14	11
For party unity should support Turner	10	12	9	10	11
I like Turner	10	5	9	8	10
Because of Turner's stand on the issues	8	14	6	10	10
Out of loyalty to the leader/Out of loyalty to Turner	5	1	3	6	7

TABLE VI

Obviously, delegates were not overwhelmingly struck by Turner's potential for winnability, nor by his stand on issues. The vote against review was motivated to a large degree by some confidence in Turner's potential as a leader, and also by the fear of the negative effect a leadership review and party division would have on the party itself and public opinion of the party. How then did the delegates perceive the John Turner they were re-endorsing as party leader? From whence did he derive support?

When Liberal delegates were asked whether Brian Mulroney and John Turner were, in turn, doing an excellent, good, fair or poor job, Mulroney scored 15 on an index of 100 points and Turner 66. Turner's greatest support came from the right-of-center Liberals (69) and Quebeckers (71). The weakest response was indicated by left-of-center Liberals (59) and former Chrétien supporters (49).

Later, questioned about the public perception of Turner, 63% of Liberal delegates indicated that he was gaining political momentum, 9% that he was losing momentum and 28% that he was neither gaining nor losing political force.

Delegates were asked in a variety of areas to compare Mulroney's strengths and performance with those of John Turner. While one can expect party members to be partisan in their choices, several interesting perspectives emerge from this data. First, the data can be used to identify delegates' perceptions of Turner's strengths and weaknesses, and of his political orientation.

Once again, in almost all areas, Turner received higher marks from older delegates, from Quebec delegates and from his 1984 supporters. Asked to rate his performance overall on a 100-point scale, delegates gave him a 66 average. Delegates age 55 and over, however, gave him an average rating of 69 (compared with 60 for those under 25). Quebec delegates gave him a 71 and his previous supporters and those who voted against a leadership review a 74. When delegates elucidated the areas in which they perceived Turner to be strong, the image of Turner as an elite-oriented, B.C./Ontario-based businessman, forceful in foreign affairs but weak in promoting strong federalism, emerged again, as the following table demonstrates.[9]

	% of Delegates		Net Difference
	Answered "John Turner"	Answered "Brian Mulroney"	
Is the more honest/sincere	92	1	91
Could best deal with corporate concentration	75	9	69
Has more leadership ability	75	15	60
Could better deal with Quebec on the Constitutional issue	67	17	50
Could better deal with Quebec's concerns	63	24	39
Is the better speaker	30	58	-28
Performs better on television	26	62	-36

TABLE VII

Party continuity is derived on one hand from policy/ideological consistency and on the other from loyalty to the leader. Potential discord was being sown on both fronts. Ideological positioning, it has been demonstrated, was to some degree out of step with Liberal policy.

The loyalty issue was also complex and made more so by the problem of the old guard. In 1986, Turner campaigned as deftly against the old guard of Keith Davey and Marc Lalonde as he had against Trudeau's backroom boys in 1984. But in addition to his negative campaign against the dark forces of the past, Turner also advanced the positive theme of making the Liberals into a democratic, open party. Delegates responded enthusiastically to this cry. The sentiment in favor of internal party reform ran deep and Turner successfully caught this wave.

The convention delegates as a whole, however, did not have blinders on. The survey data indicated that their decisive endorsement of Turner's leadership was offered without major illusions about either his strengths or his weaknesses as a leader. He was, for example, perceived by delegates as being a less-effective communicator than Brian Mulroney. Of the delgates surveyed, 58%

considered Brian Mulroney to be a better speaker and 62% believed Mulroney to be better on television. Elsewhere in the survey, when asked who would win a public debate prior to another federal election, 66% supported Turner and 20%, Mulroney. This is not an overwelming vote of confidence for a party leader, but neither is an overall ranking of 66 of 100 points when evaluating the effectiveness of a leader's performance. Clearly the delegates believed that Liberal values would supersede the leader's instincts.

Asked what would be the results of a federal election with Mulroney leading the Tories and Turner the Liberals, Liberal delegate responses were divided as follows: 3% opted for a Conservative majority, 14% a Conservative minority, 39% a Liberal majority and 38% a Liberal minority.

The delegates seemed to recognize that John Turner had his foibles as a leader, but they also believed that the Liberal party could and would win the next election with Turner at the helm. That said, the expectation of many was for a Liberal minority rather than majority victory. Delegates were prepared to accept minority government as a trade-off, prescient of possible dilemma and confusion to come.

What delegates were suggesting in their responses, in part, was already that minority government would not be catastrophic, for either the Liberal party or for the country. Liberals in Ontario were learning that minority government could work well and in some respects provide a fairer and more responsive form of government than a majority government. By giving John Turner a solid vote of confidence at a time when there was some doubt among the general public and the media about the party's chances to win the next election, the survey findings suggested that a great many Liberals were prepared to accept a Liberal minority victory as a more-than-satisfactory result in the next election. They were prepared to endorse John Turner with the understanding and expectation that the Liberals might not be able to win a majority victory under him in the next election — and this was not cause for great consternation. The delegates clearly felt that Turner had earned a second chance. They liked the way he consulted the party members and were therefore prepared to give him their support. They felt they could control his policy direction, even if they didn't feel comfortable with his policy instincts.

Clearly, the Liberal delegates surveyed wanted to win the next election, but, more importantly, they now wanted the party to return to its traditional point of view, its traditional value system predicated on historical precedents that have stood the Liberals in good stead:

*activist government;

*social welfare;

*regional economic distribution.

The Liberals learned in 1986 that the electorate by and large is pragmatic and non-ideological. People vote for issues and party policy. Canadians vote generally from self-interest and identify with the system that they perceive will "serve and protect" them best, rationalizing about policy platform as they may.

To some degree, however, Canadians do not approve of a three-party system which masquerades as a one-party system with cells differentiated by leaders with different names. When issues and orientation are not clearly defined disaster ensues for the party which has worn a "disguise" to court popularity. Like Cinderella, the Liberals in 1984 had worn Conservative make-up, but at the stroke of midnight the coaches had turned to pumpkins — and Cinderella was back in true costume.

After his election as party leader in 1984, Turner had begun to make his party nervous. As he spoke publicly about the deficit, about patronage, about the world price of oil, party members had felt their foundations begin to shake. Cognizant that some of their old values had been laid aside for the sake of winnability, and unsure of Turner's commitment to traditional Liberal values, they called the convention hoping the leadership review would bring Turner back on track.

In 1986 the Liberal party was more reserved in its optimism and less sure about its role. It was a party trying to re-define its place in the political spectrum. It was a party that wanted to return to its traditional small *l* liberal, left-of-center roots in terms of social-policy orientation. It was a party that continued to be nationalistic and that continued to support strong, centralist government. It was a party that, although humbled, was beginning to feel good about itself once again. It was less preoccupied with winning power for the sake of power, but it was also less clear about what it stood for and what it wanted for Canada.

One almost sensed that the entire Liberal party, as represented by these delegates, was reflecting on the reason they had chosen John Turner as leader in the first place. At the 1984 leadership convention, they had chosen John Turner because they thought he could win, not because of the policy direction he represented for the Liberal party. They had forsaken their values. Now guilt and Turner's promise of an open party combined to force them to try again.

It was apparent, as well, from the delegate survey data that the delegates were sending John Turner a very clear message about the kind of leadership they wanted from him, fully expecting that he would respond to their message and produce a party consistent with Liberal party tradition. Turner's position after the convention, in fact, could only be stronger since the party delegates felt they had been given a chance to make a realistic assessment of his talents and would henceforth be part of and influence the future direction and policy of the party.

Turner's answer in 1986 was a promise of a new style of personal politics built on the old Liberal value system. The new style offered dialogue, consultation, honesty and careful listening: a chastened chief offered a more humble style to a chastened party. Assured that Turner would not lead them where they did not want to go, the Liberals rallied around. They were still fearful, but the major tremors and trepidations had subsided. Although they perceived that some risk still persisted, they were prepared to take what they considered to be a lesser risk.

As 1986 faded into 1987, the challenge for the Liberals was to demonstrate a distinctive point of view — a stance different from that of the Tories and the NDP. Turner's task was continually to translate into policy for his party, his caucus and his electorate, the promises he had made, and to develop a consensus in those areas in which his party was most divided. Turner now had to demonstrate that his values and Liberal policy values were one and the same.

8

Meech Lake and Free Trade: and Who Shall Sail the Ship of State?

Some six or seven thousand Canadians chose two men to lead the Conservative and Liberal parties in 1983 and 1984; millions of Canadians would later choose Brian Mulroney to become prime minister. What has our study of these Canadians told us about the values, motivations and actions of the party activists, the least understood and most ignored component of our party system? And what connection is there between the values of these party activists and the politics of 1988?

First, Canada's two senior parties still play by brokerage rules of the game invented by Sir John A. Macdonald and perfected by William Lyon Mackenzie King. A passion to win is the most important motivation of party delegates. Because of their doubts about Joe Clark's ability to win, the Conservatives replaced him with Brian Mulroney. Because of their conviction that John Turner could win, Liberal delegates voted for him even though he was committed to taking the party down a road that most delegates did not want to follow. The two parties not only play the brokerage game by putting winning ahead of issues, they also actively try to set the party direction according to the prevailing needs of the time. Weak in Quebec, the Conservatives reached out to that province by choosing Brian Mulroney. At odds with the perceived conservative temper of the times, Liberal activists endorsed moving their party to the right. Winning power, rather than policy purity, is the dominant motif of our party system.

Yet while winning is still the name of the game, the two parties play the game for very different ends. The policy positions favored by Conservative and Liberal party activists are quite different and, on some issues they diverge radically. Electoral results may soften these differences; having won the 1984 national election, Conservative activists may have lost their antipathy to the federal government. Having won the provincial elections in Quebec, Ontario, Prince Edward Island and New Brunswick, Liberals may have gained some sympathy for the role of the provinces in our federal system. But the two parties start from very different ends of the policy spectrum and their formal names clearly describe their political convictions: the Conservative party *is* conservative and the Liberal party *does* believe in liberalism.

Ironically, this clear modern distinction between the two parties harkens back to the golden age of Macdonald and Laurier when the two parties were also clearly distinct. Today they have reversed their historical position. Like the Liberal party of the nineteeth century, modern Conservatives believe in less government, provincial autonomy and closer relations with the Americans. Like Macdonald's National Policy of 1879, modern Liberal policy advocates active government, a strong, even dominant federal power and an independent Canada distinct from the embrace of the United States. Macdonald and Laurier last squared off against one another in 1891, but their debate continues to resonate even today.

The other critical conclusion of this study is that not only do the values of Conservatives and Liberal activists differ, but also that such differences matter. The party leadership may make tactical choices based on the brokerage model, but in time the overall direction of the party reflects the core values of the most committed members. Meech Lake and free trade are a case in point.

The overwhelming consensus in the Conservative party revolves around an antipathy to government and a sympathy toward the United States. Conservatives revere the market and distrust government's efforts to distort market operations in favor of goals of equity, redistribution or nationalism. The connecting link between Meech Lake and free trade is that the two policies reduce the power of the federal government.

The logic of free trade is that the market should reign supreme and not be distorted by tariffs, regional industrial grants or cultural protection. The market must be the supreme allocator of values. Government should get out of the way.

The logic of Meech Lake, apart from giving the province of Quebec special status in Canada through the distinct society clause, is to reduce the sway of the federal government by giving the provinces the power of appointment over the Senate and the Supreme Court and to make the federal-provincial conference rather than the federal Parliament the supreme decision-making focus in the land.

Because antipathy to government forms the core of the Conservative party's value system, it should not come as a surprise that the Mulroney government has championed two policies that seek to embed this anti-government bias deep into the Canadian fabric. Whether one agrees or disagrees with this Conservative perspective, there can be little doubt that it reflects the ideological world view of Conservative activists. Mulroney is at least keeping faith with his party by promoting such a massive change. If the Conservatives succeed with their Meech Lake/free trade agenda, Canada will be a very different kind of country. But that is exactly what Conservative activists have been dreaming about for the last 20 years.

For a modern Liberal, government plays a different role. To a Liberal, the federal government is a partner, not an opponent. Government is an instrument to be employed against the powerful and self-satisfied. In this sense, the universal franchise always has had a potential for radicalism. Policies to shrink the scope of government by underfunding, undertaxing, under-regulating or over-decentralizing take away the primary means by which working men and women can better their lives. Conservatives may place their faith in self-regulatory private markets, but Liberals still dream of a Just Society.

Given this Liberal value structure, the Meech Lake Accord strikes at the heart of Liberal belief. Brian Mulroney moved in tandem with his party's deepest beliefs in forging a deal with the provinces; John Turner's endorsement of the pact repudiated his party's intrinsic heritage. Liberals would not have negotiated the Meech Lake pact. Table I indicates that a clear majority of Liberal activists would not have supported its terms.[1]

	% of Liberal Delegates
FOR FEDERAL INTERVENTION OVER PROVINCIAL OBJECTIONS IN THE ASSURANCE OF MINORITY LANGUAGE RIGHTS (1984)	**63**
or, for minority language rights to be more of a provincial matter (1984)	29
FOR MORE POWER FOR THE FEDERAL GOVERNMENT AND A STRONG CENTRAL GOVERNMENT (1984)	**78**
or for more power for the provincial governments (1984)	12
FOR A STRONGER CENTRAL GOVERNMENT WHERE THE FEDERAL GOVERNMENT TAKES CHARGE WHERE FEDERAL-PROVINCIAL CONFRONTATION OCCURS (1984)	**75**
or, for more power for provincial governments and more autonomy for them to act on their own when confrontation develops (1984)	14
FOR NOT GIVING QUEBEC A VETO OVER CONSTITUTIONAL CHANGES (1986)	**57**
or for giving Quebec a veto over constitutional changes to bring Quebec into the constitution (1986)	36

TABLE I

Why John Turner so quickly endorsed the Meech Lake Accord — before his caucus or party had the chance to debate its implications — remains a mystery. It may reflect his personal convictions, or a private understanding made with Raymond Garneau, the one prominent Quebec politician Turner had been able to attract in the 1984 debacle. More likely, however, Meech Lake is another example of the Liberal dichotomy between principle and power. Meech Lake has powerful forces behind it, Premier Robert Bourassa being the most notable. The Accord is popular in Quebec — why shouldn't it be since it gives the government of Quebec even more than it asked for? For the federal Liberal party to challenge the Quebec Liberal party over Meech Lake would mean a bitter fraternal battle over conflicting visions of federalism. Better to give in, counsel the party professionals. Who needs party division just before the next election? But if party appeasement gained peace in Quebec, it brought profound disillusionment elsewhere. Canada was denied a meaningful debate on some of the most important changes ever proposed by a federal government because the Liberal party lost faith with its past. During the Trudeau era, Joe Clark fought heartily against the patriation of the Constitution because he viewed it as dissonant with the Tory value system. His resistance gave sustenance and credibility to the Conservatives as it firmly positioned the Tory vision of where they wanted the country to go.

No real struggle took place over Meech Lake. The Tory vision won by default. The Liberal point of view — one which had been confirmed in election after election during the 1960s and 1970s — did not even receive a hearing (except for Trudeau's appearances before a joint House of Commons/Senate parliamentary committee and the Senate). Turner's acquiescence in the Conservative brand of decentralized federalism was interpreted by his party — and hence the country — as acceptance of a different concept of Canada. With one stroke, the Liberal party's traditional positioning as the advocate of strong, activist national government was traded in for a temporary peace. The result has been anxiety and internal discord within the party. Turner's leadership once again was questioned widely in the summer of 1987 after his acceptance of Meech Lake. Prominent Liberals broke with the leader's position. Party activists have been organizing against the pact outside their party framework and 11 members of the Liberal caucus split from their leader to vote against Meech Lake when it was first brought before the House of Commons. The result has been confusion in the public mind about where the Liberal party stands.

TOWARD A FEDERAL ELECTION

Is it possible that the Conservative party, which won 50% of the vote and the greatest number of seats in Canadian history in the federal election in 1984, might finish third in the next? Could it be that the Liberal party — so dominant for so many generations that commentators wearily referred to it as the "natural governing party" — might be on the road to oblivion? And most stunningly, is there a chance that the left-leaning NDP, traditionally a minority party of regional protest, might actually do as well as the two senior parties? The answer to all the above is yes.

On July 20, 1987 an NDP sweep of three federal by-elections in Newfoundland, Ontario and the Yukon confirmed what public opinion polls had been forecasting since the spring: at that moment in time, the NDP was the most popular political movement in Canada. When they gained those two seats from the Conservatives and held on to one of their own, the NDP's margin in the by-elections reflected the national trend. The New Democrats won 44.8% of the combined vote compared to 28.3% for the Liberals and 25.7% for the Conservatives. Canada appeared to be on the verge of an historic political realignment. Since their high point during the summer of 1987, the NDP has started to slip, the Conservatives have begun to come back, and the Liberals have narrowly moved ahead of their competitors. As this is being written in the spring of 1988, all three parties are in a virtual tie.

THE POST-TRUDEAU ERA

To understand the present extreme volatility of Canadian politics, where one party surges ahead only to be replaced by another six months later, we must return to the enigmatic figure of Pierre Trudeau. For 16 years prime minister of Canada, Trudeau dominated his political generation as thoroughly as Franklin Roosevelt did the Depression era of the United States. The recent turmoil in Canada is the inevitable result of Trudeau's departure in 1984.

Like Roosevelt's New Deal, the Trudeau coalition was composed of a curious amalgam of diverse elements. Quebec was the Liberal fortress: in Trudeau's last election in 1980, for example, the Liberal party won 68% of the vote in that province, taking 74 of 75 seats. With Quebec alone providing half the seats required for a majority government, the Trudeau Liberals needed only a three-way split with their Conservative and NDP competitors in English-speaking Canada to win election after election.

In addition to his appeal to Quebec as a native son, Trudeau transformed his party by attracting an almost classic social-democratic core of the young, women, ethnic supporters and the disadvantaged. Extension of the welfare state, an activist national government, anti-nuclear military policies, promotion of a Canadian Bill of Rights, and a series of measures to promote greater Canadian ownership of the economy gave the Liberals a powerful electoral combination. Such policies were not without cost. By the mid-1980s the affluent, and especially members of the business community, had deserted the Liberal party in droves, but Trudeau had successfully blunted the appeal of the NDP.

Since 1984, the subterranean theme of Canadian politics has been the dissolution of the Trudeau coalition. The Conservative party, led for the first time by a Quebecker, Brian Mulroney, attacked one pillar of Liberal support by winning 58 Quebec seats in the 1984 election. The New Democrats, led by Edward Broadbent, are now assaulting the second bastion of Liberal strength by attempting to take away the social-democratic base. Like the Roman Empire, the Liberal party in the era of Trudeau seemed to be impregnable, but, as in Rome's fall, what is truly remarkable is the speed of the collapse once its outer defenses were breached.

THE TORY PLUNGE

After 16 years of Trudeau's stormy leadership, on September 4, 1984, Canadians voted for change and the new Conservative leader, Brian Mulroney, won 211 seats — Canada's greatest electoral victory. But like a soufflé, the Tories have collapsed just as quickly as they rose. Halfway through his first term, the message of the July by-election was, in the words of a jubilant Newfoundlander, "Brian, pack your bags!"

Lack of esteem for Prime Minister Mulroney is the principal

source of the Tory decline. Since 1984 the economy has generally performed well. Three factors weaken Mulroney's appeal: two are self-inflicted wounds and the third the result of bad luck.

First, the Conservatives threw away their first year-and-a-half in office. Unlike Ronald Reagan or Margaret Thatcher, Mulroney did not come to office with a coherent plan. The finance minister was forced to retreat on his plan to cut old-age pensions, the statements of the external affairs minister were often contradicted by the prime minister, the contract system for government procurement was warped to fit regional political needs, etc. By their second year in office, the Tories had set an agenda — tax reform, free trade with the United States, decentralization of power to the provinces, but Mulroney's image as an indecisive wheeler-dealer was fixed in the public's mind.

These initial Tory stumbles can be explained by inexperience, but not so the second main difficulty: the Conservatives have flagrantly broken one of their main election themes of 1984. They had attacked the Liberals for excessive patronage and favors to their friends, and Mulroney had emphasized the point dramatically in a television debate. But soon after taking office, a series of scandals overwhelmed the government: the minister of small businesses resigned over allegations of improper real-estate deals; the minister of industry resigned over allegations of conflict of interest, and a Conservative member of Parliament was charged with influence-peddling. The list goes on. Venality was heaped onto the image of indecision.

Third, Mulroney had consistently been embarrassed by a protectionist U.S. Congress. A former CEO of the Iron Ore Company of Canada, a Canadian subsidiary of Hanna Mining of Cleveland, Mulroney came to office determined to give "the benefit of the doubt to the U.S." Relegated to the back sections of the business news in the American media, U.S. countervail duties against Canadian imports of fish, steel and timber have been front-page sensations in Canada. A June 1987 survey by Goldfarb Consultants reveals that 61% of Canadians believe that the Mulroney government has not been tough enough in its dealings with the U.S. An image of subservience only adds to the Mulroney government's woes. Ironically, U.S. trade policy may be a large factor in defeating the most pro-American prime minister in Canadian history.

THE NDP ASCENDANT

In March 1984, survival was the goal of the NDP, not government. With only 11% support in the polls at that time, there was a real chance that the party would fail to win the 12 seats needed to qualify for party status in the House of Commons.

The choice of John Turner by the Liberals gave NDP leader Edward Broadbent his opening. Painting Mulroney and Turner as two conservative peas in a pod, Broadbent won 19% of the vote in the 1984 election. Since that date, he has followed a consistent strategy of taking advantage of his opponents' mistakes while avoiding radical pronouncements. The center of the road is getting very crowded in Canada.

Broadbent's strengths are the converse of his opponents' weaknesses: never having held office, he appears more virtuous than Mulroney; heir to a social-democratic tradition, he appears more consistent than Turner. Table II shows Broadbent's dominance in the leadership stakes.[2]

Overall would you say you are impressed, a little impressed, or not at all impressed with . . .

	Mulroney		Turner	Broadbent
Impressed	18	3	25	50
A little impressed	26		26	21
Not impressed at all	53		44	22

TABLE II

Born in the prairies of the Depression era, the NDP has always had a base in Canada's West and with the Canadian labor movement. The party's success of late is largely due to a breakthrough in Quebec: Quebec voters left their Liberal roots in 1984 to vote for a Conservative native son. Disappointed with Brian Mulroney, Quebec made the NDP — at least according to the polls — a strong competitor with the old-line parties. But with a weak organization in Quebec, will the NDP be able to translate support in the polls into votes at the ballot box? The answer to that question will determine the future of Canadian politics.

If the NDP does do well at the next election, a second fascinating question emerges. Will it too adopt the brokerage (win at all costs) philosophy of its older competitors? Surveys taken at the 1983 convention of the NDP reveal that NDP activists clearly reject the brokerage thesis. With 45% of the delegates in 1983 classifying themselves as social democrats and 30% as socialists, more than three-quarters of its delegates rejected the idea that they "present a more moderate image to the general public."[3] A majority of the delegates (55.6%) wanted the NDP to move "more clearly to the left." The NDP is only now beginning to debate what it is like to be in the mainstream.

VOX POPULI: VOX DEI

As the next federal election approaches, Canadians are volatile, confused and irritable. They are not happy with the choices before them. Edward Broadbent has a wide personal dominance in comparison with Mulroney and Turner, but several NDP policy positions are anathema to Canadians. NDP party activists, for example, favor by wide margins the withdrawal of Canada from NATO and NORAD, but Canadian voters support remaining in the western alliance just as heavily. Broadbent's political trick will be to articulate Canadian concerns strongly enough to maintain his electoral advantage (send them a message), but not so strongly that the next election can be polarized around the theme of free enterprise versus socialism. His best chance for forming a government will come if no one really believes that he *will* form a government.

Brian Mulroney has to get the public to focus on free trade and Meech Lake instead of himself. He has already lost the referendum on himself (difficult though this might be for him to accept), but he still has a chance to win an issue-oriented election. In 1988, although support for the Conservative party itself languishes at about 30% in the polls, support for free trade, for example, is considerably higher, at 43%.[4] The Conservatives do relatively well on the issues, but disastrously in the leadership stakes. To win the next election, Brian Mulroney must run and hide at the same time.

But going into the next election, the NDP and Conservatives at least have one distinct advantage over their Liberal opponents. The NDP and the Tories each have a distinct approach to public policy, and voters recognize this difference. The NDP is identified with labor and social welfare; the Conservative party is perceived to promote the interests of business and the provinces. The Liberal party is not identified in the voter's mind with any distinctive policy. It was once the party of minority rights and strong national government. That image has been blurred. John Turner is opposed to free trade because it will erode Canada's national sovereignty and weaken the federal government, but he is in favor of Meech Lake, which equally decentralizes federal power and resources. As Virginia Woolf once said about California, "There is no there, there."

Hemmed in by two clear ideological alternatives and his own political inconsistency, Turner's task will be to leap-frog his opponents by re-defining the political agenda. Ralph Whitehead, a political analyst in Massachusetts, has assessed the Republican and Democratic parties in categories that apply equally well to Canada.[5] Voters see the New Democratic Party as a force with a soft heart and a tender mind. They see the Conservative party as a force with a hard heart and a tough mind. The task for the Liberal party will be to develop a program that shows it to be a party with a tough mind and a soft heart. No party has yet developed any long-lasting appeal to the baby-boom generation. No party has yet been able to articulate in a meaningful way the economic frustrations of working men and women or to offer a real solution to help the middle class survive the tide of global change washing over our economy. No party has yet captured, as part of its intrinsic appeal, the environmental, participatory and peace concerns of the post-materialist sons and daughters of the 1960s and 1970s.

Political parties are not the playthings of leaders. They have collective identities, a core clientele and, above all, institutional memory. As we approach the next federal election, each of our three parties will have a difficult time balancing the conflicting needs of the party leadership, the core of activists and the broader band of voters.

- Edward Broadbent must retain the social-democratic vision of his activist core while broadening the party's appeal to a larger constituency.

- Brian Mulroney must defend the pro-market beliefs of his Conservative party while demonstrating to skeptical Canadians that the economic gains of the market are worth more than the social upheaval the market brings.

- John Turner must take his party's values and fashion a new agenda distinctive from his opponents' and relevant to the needs of Canadians. The most difficult task belongs to John Turner.

ENDNOTES

Authors' Notes

1. For a general overview of this period see Norman Snider, *The Changing of the Guard: How the Liberals Fell from Grace and the Tories Rose to Power* (Toronto: Lester and Orpen Dennys, 1985). Those especially interested in the Conservative party should consult Patrick Martin, Allan Gregg and George Perlin, *Contenders: The Tory Quest for Power* (Scarborough, Ontario: Prentice-Hall Canada Inc., 1983) and for a veteran journalist's view of the 1984 Liberal convention see Charles Lynch, *Race for the Rose: Election 1984* (Toronto: Methuen, 1984). For an excellent academic analysis of the 1983 and 1984 leadership conventions see George Perlin, ed., *Party Democracy in Canada: The Politics of National Party Conventions* (Scarborough, Ontario: Prentice-Hall Canada Inc., 1988).

2. During the week of June 6, 1983, 1,000 delegates to the Conservative convention were interviewed. Twelve hundred delegates to the 1984 Liberal convention were sampled during the week of June 4, 1984. Then 600 Liberals were polled during the leadership convention in November 1986.

Introduction

1. Probably the best source of the ideas and character of Edward L. Bernays is found in *Biography of an Idea: Memoirs of Public Relations Counsel Edward L. Bernays* (New York: Simon and Schuster, 1965).

2. The literature of pollsters is, indeed, expanding. Many pollsters are now becoming more public figures and they are beginning to write for journals, magazines, etc. However, there is still a lack of self-reflection in most of the work of the pollsters. A valuable source of ideas is found in the journal, *Campaigns and Elections.*

3. The analogy of the pollster to the fool is most revealing. However, like the literature on the pollster, the literature on the fool is surprisingly sparse. The classic study is Enid Welsford, *The Fool: His Social and Literary History* (London: Faber and Faber, 1935). A useful further study is Paul V.A. Williams, ed., *The Fool and the Trickster: Studies in Honour of Enid Elsford* (Cambridge: D.S. Brewer Ltd., 1979). Also, by William Willeford, *The Fool and His Scepter: A Study in Clowns and Jesters and Their Audience* (Chicago: Northwestern University Press, 1969). For a good historical study of the fool, see Heather Arden, *Fools Play: A Study of Satire in the Sottie* (Cambridge: Cambridge University Press, 1980), and Olive Mary Busby, *Studies in the Development of the Fool in the Elizabethan Drama* (Oxford: Oxford University Press, 1923).

Chapter 1

1. Edmund Burke, "On the Present Discontents," in *Government, Politics and Society,* ed. B.W. Hill (Glasgow: Fontana/The Harvester Press, 1975), 113.

2. Quoted in Maurice Duverger, *Political Parties: Their Organization and Activity in the Modern State.* Trans: Barbara and Robert North (New York: John Wiley and Sons, Inc., 1951), Preface xiv.

3. See Gad Horowitz, "Towards the Democratic Class Struggle," in Trevor Lloyd and Jack McLeod, eds. *Agenda 70* (Toronto: University of Toronto Press, 1968) and William Christian and Colin Campbell, *Political Parties and Ideologies in Canada* (Toronto: McGraw-Hill Ryerson, 1974).

4. Donald V. Smiley, "The National Party Leadership Convention," in *Canadian Journal of Political Science* (December 1968), 390.

5. Harold D. Clarke, Jane Jenson, Lawrence LeDuc and Jon H. Pammett, *Absent Mandate: The Politics of Discontent in Canada* (Toronto: Gage Publishing, Ltd., 1984), 37.

6. In the most exhaustive study of voter loyalty, 63% of the electorate were classified as flexible (changing parties at least once) and 37% as durable. Between 1974 and 1980, 51% of the electorate voted 3 times for the same party, 36% switched at least once, and 25% did not vote at least once. Ibid., 57-65. This 60-40 volatility split is confirmed by private surveys.

7. The most succinct description of the role of party is found in John Meisel, "The Decline of Party in Canada," in *Party Politics in Canada,* 4th ed., ed. Hugh G. Thorburn (Scarborough, Ontario: Prentice-Hall Canada, Ltd., 1979), 119-135.

8. A good account of the institution is found in John C. Courtney, *The Selection of National Party Leaders in Canada* (Toronto: MacMillan, 1973).

9. The June 1984 survey for CTV forecast a second ballot result of 53% Turner, 40% Chrétien and 7% Johnson. The actual percentages were 54%, 40% and 6%.

Chapter 2

1. V.O. Key, *The Responsible Electorate* (Cambridge, Mass: Harvard University Press, 1966), 30.

2. Richard Johnston, "Party Alignment and Re-Alignment in Canada," unpublished PhD thesis, Stanford (1975), 20.

3. The most comprehensive studies of recent Canadian elections are contained in Harold D. Clarke, Jane Jenson, Lawrence LeDuc and Jon Pammett, *Political Choice in Canada* (Toronto: McGraw-Hill Ryerson, 1979) and *Absent Mandate* (Toronto: Gage Publishing Ltd., 1984).

4. Using different measures of volatility, analysts dispute the exact number of party tranformations. See Donald Blake, "1896 and All That," *Canadian Journal of Political Science* (June 1979) and Richard Johnston, "Federal and Provincial Voting," in David Elkins' and Richard Simeon's *Small Worlds* (Toronto: Methuen, 1980). For a useful overview see John Terry's and Brooke Jeffrey's "Transformations of the Federal Party System," an unpublished paper presented to the Canadian Political Association Meeting, 1983.

5. The six eras in Canadian party history are summarized in the following charts:

**Macdonald Conservatism 1867-
Confederation (50:1); antis (49)**

**Era 1
1867-1891**

	Liberal	Conservative	Characteristics
1872	49.1	49.9	Emergence of party politics in Canada. Alliance between Loyalist Tories, business, and Bleu French-Canadian faction dominates Liberal coalition of Clear Grit reformers and Rouges of Quebec, especially after National policy of 1878.
1874	53.8	45.4	
1878	46.3	52.5	
1882	46.8	50.7	
1887	48.1	50.2	
1891	47.1	51.1	

**Golden Era of Two-party
Competition**

**Era 2
1896-1911**

	Liberal	Conservative	Characteristics
1896	45.1	46.1	Laurier's breakthrough in Quebec makes French-Canadian support the most important component of the Liberal party. Laurier Liberals win four straight elections, and lose 1911 on a narrow swing of 2%. Critical elections in 1896 and 1900 and maintaining elections thereafter.
1900	51.2	47.4	
1904	52.0	46.4	
1908	50.4	46.9	
1911	47.7	50.1	

Politics in Transition

Era 3
1917-1930

	Liberal	Conser-vative	Pro-gressive	Characteristics
1917	Union coalition (48.4) vs. Laurier (45.5)			Three-party system emerges in 1921, but Progressives gradually merge into Liberal party or form
1921	40.7	30.3	22.9	left-wing ginger group.
1925	39.9	46.5	8.9	Conservatives dominate in
1926	46.1	45.3	5.3	Ontario; Liberals in Quebec
1930	45.2	48.8	2.8	and Maritimes are competitive.

The King Coalition

Era 4
1935-1953

	Liberal	Conser-vative	CCF	Social Credit	Characteristics
1935	44.8	29.6	8.8	4.1	Depression shatters the Conservatives and a four-party
1940	51.5	30.7	8.5	2.7	system emerges. Liberal party
1945	40.9	27.4	15.6	4.1	adopts social security and
1949	49.5	29.7	13.4	2.3	Keynes. Canada moves into the
1953	48.8	31.0	11.3	5.4	industrial age.

The Diefenbaker Realignment

Era 5
1957-1965

	Liberal	Conser-vative	CCF/NDP	Social Credit	Characteristics
1957	40.9	30.9	10.7	6.6	Diefenbaker shifts center of Conservative party from
1958	33.6	53.6	9.5	2.6	Ontario to the West. Social
1962	37.2	37.3	13.5	11.7	Credit emerges as a third party
1963	41.7	32.8	13.1	11.9	in Quebec. Liberals become
1965	40.2	32.4	17.9	3.7	part of urban Canada and NDP forms an alliance with labor.

The Trudeau Era

Era 6 1968-1980	Liberal	Conser- vative	NDP	Social Credit	**Characteristics**
					Four-party system becomes
					three as Social Credit melds
1968	45.5	31.4	17.0	4.4	into Conservatives in the
1972	38.5	35.0	17.7	7.6	West and Liberals in Quebec.
1974	43.2	35.4	15.4	5.1	Regionalism becomes more
1979	40.1	35.9	17.9	4.6	pronounced with Liberals
1980	44.3	32.5	19.8	1.7	dominant in Quebec, Conser-
					vatives in the West and Ontario
					as the swing province.

6. Succinct descriptions of Canada's elections are found in J. Murray Beck, *Pendulum of Power: Canada's Federal Elections* (Scarborough, Ontario: Prentice-Hall, 1968).

7. In contrast with Laurier, Diefenbaker made a comparable breakthrough in Quebec in 1958, winning almost 50% of the vote and gaining 50 seats to the Liberals' 15. But in 1962 his vote total in Quebec fell to 29% and only 14 Conservatives were returned. In Quebec, 1958 was a deviating, not a critical election. Similarly in 1968, Pierre Trudeau increased Liberal representation in the North and the West to 28 members from 9 in 1965. But in 1972 this fell back to 7.

8. Johnston, "Party Alignment," 15.

9. The strength of the Conservatives in the Prairies during this period is demonstrated by the following table (Source: Beck, *Pendulum of Power*):

	Prairie Support 1953-1963									
	1953		1957		1958		1962		1963	
	Seats	%	Seats	%	Seats	%	Seats	%	Seats	%
Liberal	17	37.5	6	28.2	—	18.1	2	24	3	26.1
Conservative	6	17	14	28.6	47	56.2	42	44.9	41	47
CCF/NDP	14	25.3	15	21.5	1	16.9	2	16.1	2	13.1
Social Credit	11	18.1	13	21.3	—	8.6	2	14.7	2	13.6

10. The tables which follow show clearly the support demonstrated by the young, Roman Catholics, Francophones, "ethnics" and urban dwellers for the Liberals (Sources: Reports of the Canadian Institute of Public Opinion and Goldfarb Consultants):

	Support for the Liberal Party Selected Demographic Categories 1953-1980					
	1953	1965	1968	1974	1979	1980
Sex						
Male	—	42	45	43	43	43
Female	—	43	48	43	43	46
Age						
Under 30	45	45	53	46	38	49
30-49	—	44	48	44	41	45
50+	39	40	42	38	40	40
Religion						
Roman Catholic	—	57	57	60	—	—
Protestant	—	32	38	35	—	—
Other	—	47	47	52	—	—
Community						
Over 100,000	—	46	52	46	44	50
10,000-1,000,000	—	45	42	47	39	42
Under 10,000	—	—	41	39	35	37

	Support for the Liberal Party Selected Demographic Categories 1953-1980					
	1953	1965	1968	1974	1979	1980
Labor						
Union	46	39	46	44	38	47
Non-Union	42	46	47	43	41	44
Education						
Elementary	40	46	44	44	47	46
Secondary	46	41	46	41	39	44
University	41	49	60	50	36	42
Ethnicity						
English	38	39	46	40	31	36
French	53	55	53	60	59	67
Other	—	43	44	49	47	42

11. The table which follows demonstrates the strong support of baby boomers for the Liberal party (Source: Reports of the Canadian Institute of Public Opinion):

Year	Party Support of Canadians Under 30 1968-1980			
	Party			
	Liberal Party	Conservative Party	NDP	Social Credit Party
1968	53	26	14	7
1972	47	23	20	10
1974	46	28	20	6
1979	38	33	20	9
1980	49	22	27	3

12. Clarke, LeDuc et al., *Political Choice*, 361-262.

13. Source: Election figures are summarized in Beck, *Pendulum of Power* and Howard R. Penniman, ed., *Canada at the Polls, 1979 and 1980: A Study of the General Elections* (Washington: American Enterprise Institute, 1981).

	Sources Of Social Credit Strength					
	1965 and 1980					
	British Columbia		Alberta		Quebec	
	1965	1980	1965	1980	1965	1980
Liberal	30	22.2	22.4	22.2	45.6	68.2
Conservative	19.2	41.5	46.6	64.9	21.3	12.6
NDP	32.9	35.3	8.3	10.3	12.0	9.1
Social Credit	17.4	.1	22.5	1.0	17.5	5.9

14. Meisel reports that in 1968, those who described themselves as upper class composed 8% of the sample but were 10% of the Liberal party's base; middle income Canadians were 48% of the sample and made up 51% of Liberal support; lower income Canadians were 44% of the sample but made up only 39% of Liberal support. According to Meisel's sample, nearly 70% of those who classified themselves as upper income voted Liberal with only 22% voting for the Conservatives and 6% for the NDP. See John Meisel, *Working Papers on Canadian Politics* (Montreal: McGill-Queen's University Press, 1975). In particular, see Tables I and II in the appendix, 285-289.

15. Support for the Liberals is clearly indicated by the figures below, indicating party affiliation between 1965 and 1980 (Source: Penniman, *Canada at the Polls, 1979 and 1980*, 61, 373):

	Party Affiliation				
	1965 to 1980				
	1965	1968	1974	1979	1980
Liberal	37	45	46	36	40
Conservative	25	23	22	21	23
NDP	11	10	10	11	14
Social Credit	6	4	3	3	3
Other	1	2	—	1	1
None	20	16	20	27	20

Chapter 3

1. At the 1983 Conservative convention 3,131 delegates were entitled to attend and 3,006 were actually accredited. At the Liberal convention a year later, 3,523 were entitled to attend and 3,442 were accredited. The roughly 100 no-shows may have been due to illness, lack of interest among ex officios or reluctance to pay the relatively large delegate fee of approximately $500.

	1983 Conservative	1984 Liberal
Entitled	3,131	3,523
Accredited	3,006	3,442
First ballot vote	2,988	3,435

2. Quoted in L. Ian MacDonald, *Mulroney: The Making of the Prime Minister* (Toronto: McCelland and Stewart, 1984), 11.

3. Martin et al., *Contenders*, 28.

4. The Conservative constitution prior to 1983 allowed a leadership review vote at general meetings held at two-year intervals. A vote of 50% plus 1 was necessary for a leadership convention to be called. The Liberal party's constitution calls for a leadership review vote to be held at the first general meeting after a federal election. In 1983, no doubt to the considerable relief of Mr. Mulroney, the Conservatives changed their constitution to allow leadership review votes to be held only after a federal election which the Conservative party has *lost*. Pierre Trudeau's return to the Liberal leadership after his resignation in November 1979 also reflects the dual monarchy principle. Trudeau consented to run in the next campaign as Liberal leader when the Conservatives were defeated in the House of Commons on December 13, 1979 only after being requested by both the caucus and the national executive of the Liberal party.

5. George C. Perlin, ed., *Party Democracy in Canada: The Politics of National Party Conventions* (Scarborough, Ontario: Prentice-Hall Canada, 1988), 86. Forty-eight percent of Conservative delegates and 41% of Liberals identified with a particular candidate, but only 39% of the Tories and 38% of Liberal delegates ran as part of a slate.

6. Martin et al., *Contenders*, 127. Clark's organization was sufficiently strong to mount slates in seven provinces. Clark and Mulroney went head to head in Quebec and Clark's slate went up against Pocklington in Edmonton and Calgary, and against Wilson in Toronto.

7. Ibid, 35.

8. The breakdown of ex officio Conservative delegates in 1983 was as follows:

Ex officio Conservative Delegates 1983

Members of Parliament, senators and official candidates	284
National executive and other nationally appointed positions	135
Members of the provincial legislature	307
Provincial appointments and delegates at large	193
Total	**919**

9. George C. Perlin, *The Tory Syndrome: Leadership Politics in the Progressive Conservative Party* (Montreal: McGill-Queen's Press, 1980), 186-187.

10. Robert Krause, Lawrence LeDuc, "Voting Behavior and Electoral Strategies in the Progressive Conservative Leadership Convention of 1976," *Canadian Journal of Political Science* (March 1979), 113. 71% of Mulroney's delegates supported Clark, as did 93% of MacDonald's; 63% of Horner's went to Wagner as did 57% of Hellyer's.

11. For an entertaining account of the 1976 convention see Patrick Brown, Robert Chodos and Rae Murphy, *Winners and Losers: The 1976 Tory Leadership Convention* (Toronto: James Lorimer and Co., 1976).

12. Perlin, *The Tory Syndrome*, 182.

13. Martin et al., *Contenders*, 9.

14. These data are compiled from findings contained in Perlin, *The Tory Syndrome*, 175-176; and the Goldfarb CTV survey of Conservative delegates, May 1983.

15. Figures contained in Perlin, *The Tory Syndrome*, 174: a November 1, 1982 party press release for the Progressive Conservative Association of Canada on the results of a survey of delegates in a May 1982 policy convention. The wording of the question was "In comparison with the average Progressive candidate, would you say your views on economic issues are: to the right, about the same as, to the left": Martin, et al., *Contenders*, 199, and CTV Goldfarb Survey, May 1983.

16. Krause and LeDuc, "Voting Behaviour in Conservative Leadership Conventions of 1976," 128.

17. Martin et al., *Contenders*, 199.

18. CTV Goldfarb survey, May 1983.

19. Ibid.

20. Ibid.

21. On the first ballot, 47% of the delegates from Quebec supported Clark, 47% Mulroney and 1% Crosbie. The regional and age breakdown was as follows:

First Ballot Support

	Clark	**Mulroney**	**Crosbie**
Total	37	25	20
Region			
West	42	22	16
Ontario	30	20	23
Quebec	47	47	1
Atlantic	29	13	45
Age			
Under 25	38	29	21
25-44	30	28	21
45+	44	19	19

(Source: CTV Goldfarb survey, May 1983.)

22. The convention vote was as follows:

	June 11, 1983			
	Ballot 1	Ballot 2	Ballot 3	Ballot 4
Clark, Joe	1,091	1,085	1,058	1,325
Mulroney, Brian	874	1,021	1,036	1,584
Crosbie, John	639	781	858	
Wilson, Michael	144	—		
Crombie, David	116	67		
Pocklington, Peter	102	—		
Gamble, John	17	—		
Fraser, Neil	5	—		

23. Martin et al., *Contenders*, 102.

24. CTV Goldfarb survey, May 1983.

25. George Perlin, Allen Sutherland and Marc Desjardins, "The Impact of Age Cleavage on Convention Politics," in *Party Democracy in Canada*, 198.

26. CTV Goldfarb survey, May 1983.

27. Ibid.

28. MacDonald, *Mulroney*, 18.

29. Ibid., 196.

Chapter 4

1. According to the Goldfarb survey of 1,200 delegates taken from the CTV polls during the week of June 4, 1984, 73% of the delegates thought the chances of the Liberal party forming the next majority government were excellent or good, only 17% thought the chances good that the party would be the official opposition.

2. Data from the Goldfarb Consultants surveys, conducted nationally 1983/1984.

3. Despite the Liberal party's long history of success, books about the party are few. Reginald Whitaker's *The Government Party: Organizing and Financing the Liberal Party of Canada 1930-58* (Toronto: University of Toronto Press, 1979) examines the King-St. Laurent era; Joseph Wearing, like Whitaker, concentrates on relations within the extra-parliamentary party and continues the analysis to the 1980s. See Joseph Wearing, *The L-Shaped party: The Liberal Party of Canada 1958-1980* (Toronto: McGraw-Hill Ryerson, 1981). Christina McCall-Newman's *Grits: An Intimate Portrait of the Liberal Party* (Toronto: MacMillan, 1982) is a fascinating look at the personalities of the party during the Pearson-Trudeau era, and J.W. Pickersgill's *The Liberal Party* (Toronto: McClelland and Stewart, 1962) is written within the perspective of a key Liberal from the King-St. Laurent era.

4. Roy MacLaren, *Consensus: A Liberal Looks at his Party* (Oakville: Mosaic Press, 1984), 164.

5. John Roberts, *Agenda for Canada* (Toronto: Lester & Orpen Dennys, 1985), 65.

6. The male/female delegate breakdown at the 1984 Liberal convention was as follows:

Male and Female Delegates, 1984

	Riding Delegates	Youth	Ex Officio	Total
Male	872	498	790	2,060
Female	868	264	150	1,413
Total	1,740	762	940	3,473

7. CTV Goldfarb survey, June 1984.

8. Ibid.

9. Ibid.

10. Ibid.

11. See J. Lele, G.C. Perlin and H.G. Thorburn, "The National Party Convention," in *Party Politics in Canada: Fourth Edition*, ed. Hugh G. Thorburn (Scarborough, Ontario: Prentice-Hall of Canada, Ltd., 1979), 77-88. This article compares the findings of 3,000 completed questionaires gathered in post-convention mailings to delegates from the 1967 Conservative convention, the 1968 Liberal convention and 1971 NDP convention. The above article contains data on the personal characteristics of party activists and many of the findings on the policy preference of Conservative delegates were published by George Perlin in *The Tory Syndrome*. The data on the Liberal delegates published in Table IV has kindly been made available by Professors Thorburn and Perlin.

12. William Christian and Colin Campbell, *Political Parties and Ideologies in Canada* (Toronto: McGraw-Hill Ryerson, 1974), 62, 63.

13. CTV Goldfarb survey, June 1984.

14. Ibid.

15. The very day that Pierre Trudeau resigned, February 29, 1984, the CBC's "Journal" — the most important news show in Canada — ran a documentary about Turner that anointed him as the next leader. The effect of this media splurge on other potential leadership aspirants was significant. See Jean Chrétien, *Straight from the Heart* (Toronto: Key Porter Books, 1985), 198.

16. Jack Cahill, *John Turner: The Long Run* (Toronto: McClelland & Stewart, 1984), 123.

17. Peter Regenstrief reports that in 1968, 61% thought the alternation tradition existed and 28% did not; 29% of the delegates thought it a good idea (45% of the French-speaking delegates and 30% of the French-speaking population thought it was a good idea). See Peter Regenstrief, "Note on the Alternation of the French and English Leaders in the Liberal Party of Canada," *Canadian Journal of Political Science* (March 1969), 118-122.

18. Lele, Perlin and Thorburn, "National Party Convention Study," unpublished paper, Queen's University, 1970.

19. CTV Goldfarb survey, June 1984.

20. Ibid.

21. Janine Brodie, "The Gender Factor and National Leadership Conventions in Canada," in *Party Democracy in Canada*, 184.

22. Ian Stewart, "The Brass Versus the Grass: Party Insiders and Outsiders at Canadian Leadership Conventions," in *Party Democracy in Canada*, 152.

23. Ibid., 153.

24. CTV Goldfarb survey, June 1984.

25. Ibid.

26. The convention results were as follows:

Ballots, Liberal Leadership Convention — June 16, 1984

	First Ballot	Second Ballot
John Turner	1,593	1,862
Jean Chrétien	1,067	1,368
Don Johnson	278	192
John Roberts	185	—
Mark MacGuigan	135	—
John Munro	93	—
Eugene Whelan	84	—
To Win	1,718	—

27. CTV Goldfarb survey, June 1984.

28. Ibid.

Chapter 5

1. Conservative party headquarters released regional breakdowns for only 3,025 delegates since some of the ex officios did not put down provincial designation. Percentages do not exactly make up 100% because of rounding.

Regional Delegate Breakdown
1983 Conservative and 1984 Liberal Conventions

	Number of Conservative Delegates	%	Number of Liberal Delegates	%
West & North	**902**	**29%**	**1011**	**29%**
British Columbia	246	8%	335	10%
Alberta	276	9%	245	7%
Saskatchewan	127	6%	191	6%
Manitoba	155	5%	170	5%
N.W. Territories	25	1%	44	1%
Yukon	23	1%	26	1%
Ontario	**904**	**29%**	**1054**	**31%**
Quebec	**742**	**24%**	**836**	**24%**
Atlantic	**527**	**17%**	**541**	**16%**
New Brunswick	135	4%	198	6%
Nova Scotia	154	5%	168	5%
P.E. Island	67	2%	76	2%
Newfoundland	171	6%	99	3%
Total	**3075**		**3442**	

2. CTV Goldfarb survey, May 1983.

3. CTV Goldfarb survey, June 1984.

4. Lele, Perlin, Thorburn, "National Party Convention," unpublished paper, Queen's University, 1970.

5. CTV Goldfarb survey, May 1983 and June 1984.

Chapter 6

1. Goldfarb Consultants, 1984 survey.

2. Goldfarb Consultants, 1983 survey.

Chapter 7

1. CTV Goldfarb survey, November 1986.

2. CTV Goldfarb surveys, May 1983, June 1984 and November 1986.

3. Liberal Party of Canada, Policy resolutions passed by the plenary session at the 1986 national convention, Ottawa 1986.

4. CTV Goldfarb survey, November, 1986.

5. Ibid.

6. Ibid.

7. Ibid.

8. Ibid.

9. Ibid.

Chapter 8

1. CTV Goldfarb survey, November 1986.

2. Goldfarb Consultants, June 1987.

3. Alan Whitehorn, "The New Democratic Party in Convention," in Perlin, ed., *Party Democracy in Canada,* 272-301.

4. Goldfarb Consultants, *Toronto Star* poll, January 1988.

5. Quoted in Rober Kuttner, *The Life Of The Party: Democratic Prospects in 1988 and Beyond* (New York: Viking/Penguin 1987), 110.